LOVE LANGUAGE
of the SOUTH

LOVE LANGUAGE
of the SOUTH

A CELEBRATION OF THE FOOD,
THE HOSPITALITY, AND THE STORIES OF
MY SOUTHERN HOME

STACY LYN HARRIS

Copyright © 2024 by Stacy Lyn Harris
Cover design by Kara Klontz. Cover photo © Mary Harris. Cover copyright © 2024 by Hachette Book Group, Inc.

Hachette Book Group supports the right to free expression and the value of copyright. The purpose of copyright is to encourage writers and artists to produce the creative works that enrich our culture.

The scanning, uploading, and distribution of this book without permission is a theft of the author's intellectual property. If you would like permission to use material from the book (other than for review purposes), please contact permissions@hbgusa.com. Thank you for your support of the author's rights.

Worthy
Hachette Book Group
1290 Avenue of the Americas, New York, NY 10104
worthypublishing.com
twitter.com/worthypub

First Edition: March 2024

Worthy is a division of Hachette Book Group, Inc. The Worthy name and logo are trademarks of Hachette Book Group, Inc.

The publisher is not responsible for websites (or their content) that are not owned by the publisher.

Worthy Books may be purchased in bulk for business, educational, or promotional use. For information, please contact your local bookseller or the Hachette Book Group Special Markets Department at special.markets@hbgusa.com.

Scripture quotations are from the King James Version of the Holy Bible.

Print book interior design by Ashley Prine, Tandem Books.

Photographs on pages 2, 4, 13, 25, 57, 68, 71, 89, 98, 106, 108, 111, 129, 142, 165, 191, 202, 204, 211, 219, 223, 250, 251, 253, 262 by Graylyn Harris.

Photographs on pages 180, 181, 217, 254 by High 5 Productions.

All other photographs by Stacy Lyn Harris.

Library of Congress Control Number: 2023941319

ISBNs: 978-1-5460-0426-4 (hardcover), 978-1-5460-0427-1 (ebook)

Printed in China

1010

10 9 8 7 6 5 4 3 2 1

For my family, who are my lifeblood. You will never know how eternally grateful I am for you all to be a part of my life. And for my Granny Effie Gray for sharing her Love Language with me and teaching me to share it with others.

Contents

Introduction

When I started writing this book, I thought that I'd be doing it purely for you all to enjoy, but as I wrote and cooked and remembered (and wrote and cooked and remembered some more) something very different ended up happening. Don't get me wrong—this book is an invitation to every twist and turn that is the roller-coaster ride of growing up in the South. You'll get to enjoy soul food with me, journey to farmers' markets and fish fries, and feel the warm embrace—and sometimes stern talking-to—of a momma's love. I just wasn't expecting to be on the roller coaster along with you! What memories, what emotions, what *therapy* . . . but now I wonder, what else did I expect? Food is the thread that binds me to my past and my present. To cook the dishes that have my heart means I've got to travel the full length of that thread. I did it just the same way as I've lived my life: With a whole lot of faith. And trust. And sweet tea.

As you journey through this book, I want to introduce you to some of the most special people in my life, take you to some of my favorite places, and share a few celebrations and memories that have sparked my imagination in the kitchen. I want to greet you on my front porch, invite you in for a freshly baked Bacon Cheddar Biscuit with Bacon Jam, and share the secret to making a mile-high meringue. I want you to know what I love about the South and why I love it, with the hope you will love it too.

Many times while writing this book, I thought of my husband. Hunters spend hours in solitude, leaving early in the morning before the roosters get up, all in hope of bringing something home for their families to eat. As a young wife fresh out of my marriage gown, I had conflicting thoughts about letting my husband leave for almost the entire day, just to eat some strange type of meat I wasn't really used to eating. But I learned to be supportive, and boy did it pay off, and in much bigger ways than Red Pepper Jelly–Basted Grilled Quail with Caramelized Peaches and Figs or Applewood Bacon–Wrapped Venison Steaks. That is how this book came together too. When I doubted, I leaned in harder.

And it's like what my mom would always say—if it's easy, maybe it's not worth doing. (Of course, she wasn't talking about my Ambrosia recipe. That's easy *and* worth doing anytime the craving strikes.) I've done enough living that I don't expect life to be 100 percent peaceful, but I do know there can always be beauty among the chaos. The most beautiful slice of Coconut Cream Pie can be born in a kitchen full of sloppy mixing bowls

on a table littered with coconut shavings and random spots of pie filling. A big bucket of dirty crawdads brought from the creek can be cleaned, shelled, and cooked into a delicious pan of mac and cheese in a small cabin kitchen with four kids lending helping hands!

I want my kitchen and home to be a. sanctuary for my family and friends. A place they can pour out their hearts as I pour them a glass of peach iced tea and serve a slice of Old-Fashioned Pound Cake that had been waiting patiently just for them in the freezer.

I want people to gather around my table telling stories, sharing countless Sunday dinners, and enjoying celebrations.

I don't go to my home and kitchen expecting perfection. It's simply the place I return to that matters most: my family, my faith, and spending my days at home in the South. Time spent cooking is time spent loving. Cooking is my love language. It's the language I know best, and if you're willing to put up your feet and stay a while, I'd like to share it with you. Come in. Make yourself at home. Let's get cookin'.

LOVE LANGUAGE
of the SOUTH

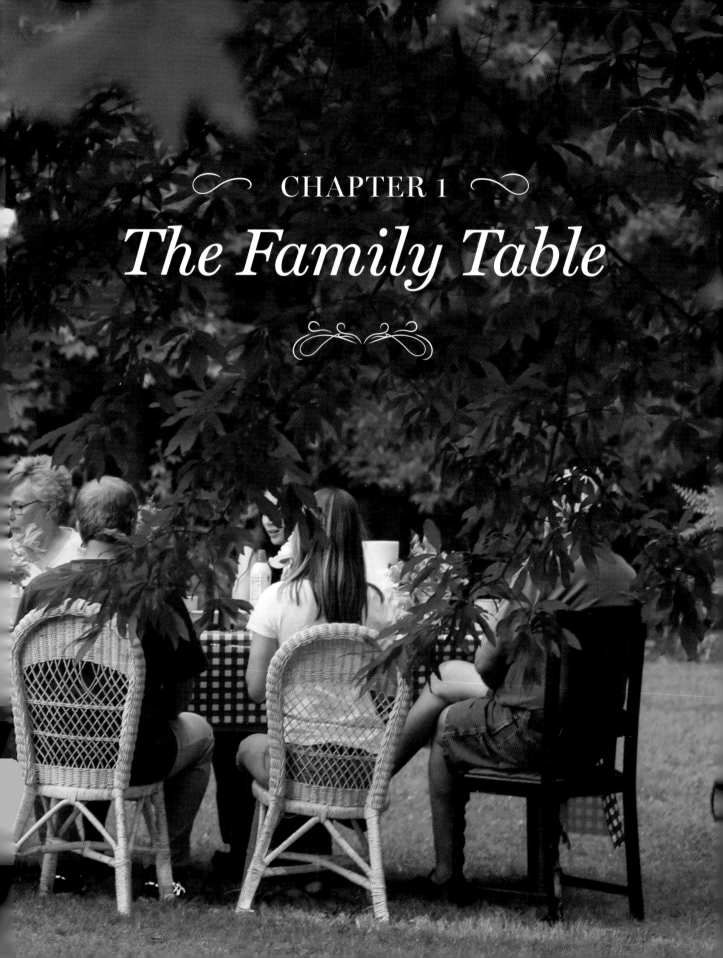

CHAPTER 1

The Family Table

Southern food represents love, comfort, peace, safety—especially around the family table. Gathering around the family table is an invitation: *Leave your baggage, problems, and insecurities at the door, and enjoy a safe place to recoup nourishment for your body and soul.*

Every gathering in the South includes food. From Sunday dinners to the wonderfully chaotic evening meals drinking sweet tea while lingering over a classic "meat and three," like fried chicken, squash casserole, fried green tomatoes, and crispy fried onion rings, followed by caramel cake. Even the cleanup has an element of belonging, joy, thankfulness, thoughtfulness— everything the South represents.

commitment to family dinner, a day doesn't pass that we haven't read each other's moods, tone, feelings, or thoughts. It is where we gauge if someone needs a little extra love or attention. It's a place to have fun, too! Ever since our children were small, we've assigned them the task of bringing one fact they don't think anyone will know to the table. The facts have been funny, educational, or just plain interesting. Boy, have we learned a lot about the world around us and about the one sharing the fact!

I know one Southern family who takes the family table to the max. They've surrounded their table with luxurious office chairs to make lingering more appealing and comfortable.

Gathering around the family table is an invitation: *Leave your baggage, problems, and insecurities at the door, and enjoy a safe place to recoup nourishment for your body and soul.*

Inescapably, the traditions around the table become a part of the Southern soul. "You're going to be here tonight for dinner, right?" isn't really a question. It's a reminder to keep first things first; a priority above all priorities. There is never a reason to break the family table tradition . . . ever! Being there each week is just as much an act of love as the cooking and serving. For those who aren't as apt to express their love verbally, grilling burgers and frying fries are as good as saying "I love you to the moon and back."

The family table is a place to truly know and understand those you love. By having a standing

This is perfect for those Sunday dinners when the braise needs just a little longer or the pie needs a few more minutes in the oven. Reminiscing, laughing, and sharing stories while waiting on the food or cleaning up builds memories and strengthens bonds.

Keeping the tradition of the family table alive is an intentional way to connect, and to give comfort, belonging, and love. Bringing every generation together, being all inclusive, enjoying delicious food with safe people in a welcoming place revives the weariest soul. It fills one with hope, thankfulness, and strength. That's why it's such a big part of life in the South.

Granny's Kitchen

My earliest food memories begin at my granny's kitchen table, which was of course covered by that familiar red-and-white plastic tablecloth you'd see in so many midcentury American homes. It seems fitting that I start this book at her tableside in that tiny little kitchen. When I close my eyes, I can still see Granny standing over the stove, donning her favorite apron, sweating over butter beans as she stirs with her left hand (she passed her left-handedness down to my dad, me, and four brought us all together and, if even for a moment, took that barrier down.

There's no doubt in my mind that Granny's cooking made the difference. Walking through the door, you'd be hit with the wafting scent of fried chicken, butter beans, creamed corn (my favorite), mashed potatoes and gravy, vegetable soup (always with meat in it!), and fried cornbread. Her home was tiny, and her air-conditioning wall unit never seemed to work, but it still felt like heaven on earth in

> *A grandparent's love can change the world.*
> *When I call to remembrance the unfeigned faith that is in thee,*
> *which dwelt first in thy grandmother Lois, and thy mother*
> *Eunice; and I am persuaded that in thee also.*
> 2 Timothy 1:5

of my seven kids). At three years old, I'd watch her cook like other kids watched cartoons.

I didn't know it then, but my dad had come home from Vietnam a very different man than when he left. My parents had married right after high school, and almost immediately after he was shipped off to fight in the war. His platoon spent their entire thirteen months in the DMZ—the hot spot in the Vietnam War. Most of his original platoon did not return home, and those who did had trouble adjusting to life back home after seeing so much death. It was hard for my dad, and he put up a barrier between himself and the rest of the world, including my mom and me. Granny's kitchen that Alabama kitchen. Her kitchen provided an intoxicating air of togetherness and comfort that touched all of us.

Every time I'd come into Granny's house, I would make a beeline over to give her a hug (that was the law) and then slyly steal one of the hoe cakes draining on the paper towel by the edge of the stove. Then I'd sit at the table and fill my plate with creamed corn—and nothing else. Why eat anything else when you've got the best, and Granny's creamed corn *was* the best. Of course, Granny indulged me, thinking I could do no wrong, even at the risk of starting World War III with my dad. He would insist I needed to eat more than just

cornbread and creamed corn, and she would counter with "It's perfectly fine," while handing my dad his heaping plate with plenty of the corn dishes.

Granny really couldn't deny me anything. She did more than just indulge me—oftentimes she'd just about go to the ends of the earth to please me. She even let me jump off the roof a time or two. When I was a teenager, she took me to the state capital and the state archives museum a few times. She probably didn't realize it, but that's when my dreams of becoming a senator began. I wanted to be part of the world she introduced me to, and later, when I was studying law, I was just pursuing an ambition that my granny cultivated in me. It's true my life has taken wonderfully different

turns, but that inspiration still resides in me. Life ain't over yet, and if my granny taught me anything, I still know I can do anything I want.

Don't underestimate the love of a grandmother. Grannies can change the world through their unconditional love and adoration of their grandkids shown right at the family table. That love can affect generations. Because of Granny's conversations with me (as she diligently poured herself into frying the mouthwatering chicken and cornbread and bringing our family together), I was filled with confidence, peace, and assurance that everything would be okay. Her kitchen was a safe place and one of empowerment; Granny's table is where great things happen, and great men and women are made.

GRANNY'S SOUTHERN FRIED CHICKEN
❦ *Serves 5–7* ❧

FOR BRINING

1 gallon water

¼ cup kosher salt

¼ cup sugar

6–10 black peppercorns

1 bay leaf

1 (4½-pound) whole chicken, cut into 8 pieces

FOR DREDGING

2 cups buttermilk

3–4 dashes Tabasco or other hot sauce

2 cups all-purpose flour

2 tablespoons kosher salt

1 teaspoon freshly ground black pepper

½ teaspoon cayenne pepper

¼ teaspoon garlic powder

FOR FRYING

2 cups vegetable oil

¼ cup bacon drippings

To brine the chicken, combine the water, salt, and sugar in a large stockpot. Over high heat, bring the mixture to a boil, whisking until the salt and sugar are dissolved. Remove from the heat and add the peppercorns and bay leaf. Allow to cool completely, then add the chicken pieces to the brine. Cover and refrigerate for 8 hours. Drain the chicken, rinse with cold water, and pat dry.

Place a wire rack over a rimmed baking sheet for the dredged chicken awaiting frying. Place a second wire rack over a rimmed baking sheet and set aside for the cooked chicken. In a medium bowl, whisk together the buttermilk and hot sauce. In a shallow dish, combine the flour, salt, black pepper, cayenne pepper, and garlic powder.

Dip each piece of chicken first into the buttermilk mixture and then into the flour mixture; shake off any excess flour. Place the coated pieces of chicken on the wire rack.

Combine the vegetable oil and bacon drippings in a 12-inch cast iron skillet or chicken fryer and heat over high heat to 375°F. Using tongs or a slotted spoon, transfer the chicken to the clean wire rack.

Add no more than four pieces of chicken at a time to the hot oil, skin side down. Cover and cook for 6 minutes, then turn the chicken over, cover again, and cook for another 6 minutes. Uncover and cook for about 5 more minutes, until an instant-read thermometer inserted into a thigh or breast registers 165°F. Using tongs or a slotted spoon, transfer the chicken to the wire rack. Repeat to cook the remaining chicken.

Stacy Lyn's Note
If you are cooking a lot of chicken and need to keep the chicken warm, put the baking sheet and wire rack with the chicken on it in a 200°F oven until all the chicken has been cooked and you are ready to serve.

FRIED JALAPEÑO CORNBREAD,
AKA *HOT WATER CORNBREAD*
⤳ *Serves 10* ⤶

2 cups self-rising cornmeal

½ teaspoon kosher salt

1 jalapeño pepper, seeded and chopped

2–2½ cups boiling water

¼ cup bacon drippings, plus more if needed

¼ cup vegetable oil, plus more if needed

In a medium bowl, mix the cornmeal, salt, jalapeño, and 2 cups boiling water together. You'll want the consistency of thick cake batter. If it is too dry, add up to ½ cup more boiling water.

In a cast iron skillet, heat the bacon drippings and oil over high heat until almost smoking. You will know the oil is hot enough when a few drops of water sizzle when dropped into the skillet.

Drop 2 tablespoons of the cornmeal mixture into the oil and fry until a golden crust forms around the edges, about 2 minutes. Then turn and brown until the cornbread is golden on the other side, 3 to 4 more minutes. Add more oil and/or bacon drippings if the skillet becomes too dry. Transfer to a paper towel to drain and serve hot.

> **Stacy Lyn's Note**
> Make sure the oil is hot enough, or the batter will absorb the oil and you won't get that crunchy exterior and creamy interior. Also, I strongly recommend you make two batches—they disappear almost as fast as you make them!

Sunday Dinner

I don't remember when it started. I don't remember when it ended. I just remember that for years during most of my childhood, we'd eat Sunday dinner at Grandaddy's house. Everyone was there: my immediate family, my uncle, and the cousins. I'd get an adrenaline rush as soon as we turned the corner in my stepdad's red Toyota 4Runner. As soon as the car pulled up on the curb (we parked on the curb, so the driveway was clear for the others), I'd race over to one of my favorite spots on earth—the landing strip of lush green grass between my grandad's house and the neighbors. To me it

him, almost knocking his town-famous peppered burgers to the floor. Grandaddy wasn't super affectionate and was kind of quiet, like my dad. He was half Creek Indian and half Greek. His olive skin had been darkened and wrinkled by the sun, and he never tired of telling me, "Stay out of the sun, Stacy. You don't want to end up looking like this." Maybe it was because I loved him so much, I thought he was good-looking. I don't remember him telling me that he loved me, but I do remember him telling me that I look exactly like his mother. I felt that meant

Sunday dinners make memories that can last a lifetime.

was the most empowering green gymnastics mat. As my parents walked in the door, I began my tumbling pass with the imagined onlookers as my audience. Over and over again I'd tumble with the utmost precision: roundoff, back handspring, back handspring, back layout, back handspring. I felt invincible!

"Stacy, it's time to eat," my mom would call out the door, bringing me back to reality. I'd run inside through the kitchen, head straight for the blue swivel chair at the end of the den, jump in the chair, and spin until I couldn't see straight. About the time the world stopped spinning, I'd see my grandfather pulling the most amazing burgers off the grill.

The second he'd enter the door, I'd make a beeline to him and throw my arms around

something special to him, and that in turn made me feel special.

We'd all overfill our plates with simple but delicious food: hamburgers, French fries, fried pickles, and fried green tomatoes. The adults and kids would squeeze around the kitchen table to discuss my grandad's favorite topic: politics. Yes, politics was the topic of our discussions almost every week, which made for exciting conversation—mainly because no one agreed! The only thing that could get Grandaddy off the topic of politics was dessert.

Historically significant Southern desserts were always served at his house: banana pudding, coconut cream pie, ambrosia, lane cake, coconut cake, key lime pie, pineapple upside-down cake, caramel cake—and let me

tell you, the caramel cake was the real deal! The desserts were never ending, nor did I want them to be.

After dinner I would often play hide-and-go-seek with my cousins. My favorite hiding spot was way up in the top of an oak tree. I could sit up there and dream for days, until I'd hear, "Stacy, get out of that tree, there's heat lightning." Just about every Sunday there was heat lightning, and then a summer shower would move in, drawing me back indoors. Summer Sunday showers were our cue that the weekend was over and it was time to go, but I knew I'd be back next Sunday.

Those weekends have never really been over for me. When I smell a burger cooking, or I run my fingers along a rough wool fabric, I'm back on that swivel chair at Grandaddy's house waiting for him to finish my burger and feeling lucky to be by his side.

ULTIMATE BACON PEPPER BURGERS
WITH CHEDDAR AND REMOULADE
⤶ *Serves 9* ⤷

FOR THE BURGERS

1½ pounds ground chuck steak

1½ pounds ground venison loin

½ cup freshly ground black pepper, plus more for seasoning

2 tablespoons kosher salt

4 tablespoons (½ stick) unsalted butter, melted

9 brioche hamburger buns, split

9 slices sharp cheddar cheese

FOR THE REMOULADE SAUCE

1 cup homemade or good-quality store-bought mayonnaise, such as Duke's or Hellmann's

¼ cup capers

1 tablespoon grainy mustard

1 tablespoon yellow mustard

1 tablespoon Dijon mustard

Pinch of kosher salt

Refrigerator pickles

1 pound bacon, cooked

1 large Vidalia or other sweet onion, sliced thin

2 tomatoes, sliced

To make the burgers, in a large bowl, mix the meats, pepper, and salt together. Don't overmix, or the meat will get too warm and mushy. (If you are grinding your own meat, add the salt and pepper to the meat before it goes through the grinder. And keep in mind that you will need to handle the meat less with your hands in order to keep the meat from getting too warm.) Form the meat mixture into nine 1½-inch-thick patties and season each patty with a little more pepper.

Heat a grill pan or cast iron skillet over medium heat. Brush the melted butter on the insides and outsides of each bun. Place the buns, cut side down, in the pan and toast for about 1 minute. Turn the buns over and toast the other side for about 30 seconds, then transfer to a plate or cutting board, cut side up.

Turn the heat up to high. Place a wire rack over a rimmed baking sheet. Add the patties to the same pan and cook for about 1 minute, then turn the temperature back down to medium and cook for about 4 minutes. Flip the patties, place a slice of cheddar cheese on top of each, and cook for another 4 minutes. Place a dome, such as a large metal bowl, over the pan to melt the cheese quicker. When the cheddar has melted and the patties have reached desired doneness, transfer the burgers to a wire rack. For rare, the internal temperature should be 120°F to 125°F; for medium rare, 130°F to 135°F; for medium well, 150°F to 155°F.

Stacy Lyn's Note
You can use all beef chuck in this recipe if you don't have venison. Also, don't be shy with the pepper. It sounds like a lot, but the pepper is the secret to these amazing burgers!

To make the remoulade, combine the mayonnaise, capers, mustards, and salt in a food processor or blender and blend until completely smooth.

To serve, spoon a generous amount of remoulade sauce onto each bottom bun, then place some pickles and 2 slices of bacon on top of the sauce. Add a burger and another dollop of sauce, then onion and tomato slices and more pickles. Cover with the top bun.

TO GRILL THE BURGERS
If using a gas grill, heat to high. If using a charcoal grill, heat until the charcoal is glowing orange and the heat is high. After cleaning the grill grate, brush the patties with a little oil, then place them on the grill and cook for 3 minutes, or until charred, then flip, add the cheese, and continue cooking for another 4 minutes, or until the burgers reach your desired doneness.

CARAMEL CAKE
❧ *Serves 15–18* ❧

FOR THE CAKE

⅓ cup unsalted butter, softened

1 cup vegetable oil

1½ cups granulated sugar

½ cup light brown sugar, firmly packed

6 large eggs plus 2 large egg yolks, room temperature

2 tablespoons vanilla extract

3 cups cake flour

1 teaspoon baking powder

½ teaspoon kosher salt

1 cup sour cream

FOR THE CARAMEL FROSTING

1 cup (2 sticks) unsalted butter, cut into pieces

2 cups light brown sugar, firmly packed

½ teaspoon kosher salt

⅓ cup heavy cream, plus more as needed

⅓ cup milk

2 cups powdered sugar

1 teaspoon vanilla extract

Whipped cream or ice cream, for serving

Preheat the oven to 350°F. Butter (or spray) and flour three 9-inch round cake pans.

To make the cake, in the bowl of a stand mixer fitted with the paddle attachment, cream the butter, oil, granulated sugar, and brown sugar on high speed for 5 minutes, or until light and fluffy. Turn the speed down to medium and add the eggs and egg yolks, one at a time, beating until well incorporated. Add the vanilla and incorporate well.

In a medium bowl, sift together the cake flour, baking powder, and salt. Still beating on medium speed, gradually add the flour mixture alternately with the sour cream to the butter mixture, beginning and ending with the flour. Be careful not to overbeat; mix just until incorporated.

Pour the batter evenly into the prepared cake pans. Bake for about 25 minutes, until a toothpick inserted in the middle of the cake comes out with just a few crumbs. Let the cakes cool on wire racks for about 10 minutes, until they begin to pull away from the sides of the pan. Remove the cakes from the pan and place them back on the racks to cool completely.

To make the frosting, combine the butter, brown sugar, salt, heavy cream, and milk in a medium saucepan and bring to a boil over medium heat, stirring constantly. Continue to cook and stir until the caramel reaches 225°F and is amber in color, about 5 minutes. Pour the mixture into the bowl of a stand mixer fitted with the whisk attachment and allow to cool for 10 minutes.

Add the powdered sugar and vanilla and mix on high speed until the frosting looks spreadable. If the frosting is too thick, add up to 3 tablespoons more cream and continue mixing to reach the desired consistency.

To assemble, place one of the cakes on a cake stand or serving plate and spread frosting over it. Repeat with the other two layers, then spread the frosting all over the entire cake. Serve with whipped cream or ice cream.

Family Tradition

Singing at the top of my lungs Hank Williams Jr.'s "Family Tradition," wind in my face, flip-flops filling with sand, I'm having the time of my life riding toward the bay on my cousin Gerry's dune buggy to go shrimping. You know those moments you wish you could hold in a bottle, but you don't know it until way after the event has passed? That's the way my family reunions were.

My grandfather was one of eight children—seven boys and one girl—all of them loud, opinionated, and hilarious. They would sit in the yard of Uncle Richard's beach house reminiscing, picking fights,

I quickly took a huge bite of what I thought was cheese pie. Oh. My. Goodness! "Am I breathing fire? I need milk!" I shrieked. All the adults threw down their plates thinking I'd been bitten by a crab. My new friend ran like the dickens to get milk for me. My lips were on fire—maybe that is what it feels like to get lip injections. All I remember is that my lips were swollen and red until the next day. A little too late, they let me in on the secret: it was *jalapeño* cheese pie!

Watching Grandaddy and his brothers light up as they exchanged stories made

> The family table isn't always in the dining room.
> The Southerner carries it into all places (even a yard
> full of chairs). The very heart of what the family table
> demonstrates is love, grace, and acceptance.

and joking, as we kids played cards on the napping porch. While they shouted and we shuffled, in the back of our minds all of us eagerly waited for what was being cooked in the tucked-away kitchen.

"Lunch is ready!" Aunt Virginia screamed out the screen door. Oh, the thoughts that went rushing through my head: *Could I make it first in line? I hope there's enough for everyone. Of course, I just must have the shrimp and grits cakes. I don't think my plate is big enough. Wow, I'm going to get a huge piece of this cheese pie.*

me want to have a large family one day—a moment that stuck with me and guided me. The yard was packed with generations having the time of their lives. One passed out in a boat in the backyard. At the time, I thought he was taking a nap! Now I know better.

Although our family wasn't perfect, at this moment life was perfect to me. There was so much love, belonging, pride, contentment, wonderful chaos. If this motley crew could love life this much, I knew I had a lot to look forward to. What a legacy.

Thankfully, Aunt Virginia also left me with a food legacy and culture that I can pass down to my children and grandchildren one day. By the way, when I could finally taste food again that day, the shrimp had just the right spice, the cheesy grits cakes had the perfect amount of crunch and creaminess, and the two dishes are still to this day the best I have ever tasted!

CAJUN SHRIMP AND GRITS CAKES
∾ *Serves 9* ∾

FOR THE GRITS CAKES

2 cups plus 1 tablespoon water, divided

1 cup heavy cream

4 tablespoons (½ stick) unsalted butter, cut into 4 pieces

½ teaspoon kosher salt

¼ teaspoon freshly ground pepper

1 cup grits

2 cups grated Gouda or sharp cheddar cheese

8 ounces bacon (about 8 slices), cooked and chopped

2 large eggs, beaten

2 cups panko breadcrumbs

Vegetable oil, for frying

FOR THE SHRIMP

2 pounds (about 36) medium shrimp, peeled and deveined

1 tablespoon kosher salt

2 teaspoons freshly ground black pepper

1 tablespoon vegetable oil

1 red bell pepper, seeded and finely chopped

½ large Vidalia or other sweet onion, finely chopped

4 celery stalks, finely chopped

2 garlic cloves, minced

¼ cup balsamic vinegar

¼ cup champagne vinegar

2 tablespoons soy sauce

2 tablespoons Dijon mustard

FOR THE AIOLI

1 red jalapeño pepper

1 cup homemade or good-quality store-bought mayonnaise, such as Duke's or Hellmann's

2 garlic cloves, minced

Juice of ½ lemon

Pinch kosher salt

2 slices bacon, cooked and chopped, for garnish

2 green onions, chopped, for garnish

½ cup grated Parmigiano-Reggiano cheese

To make the grits cakes, line an 8 x 8-inch baking dish with parchment paper. Combine 2 cups water and the heavy cream in a Dutch oven and bring to a boil over medium-high heat. Add the butter, salt, and pepper, then slowly pour in the grits and whisk for about 1 minute. Bring the mixture back to a boil, then lower the heat and simmer for 20 minutes. Remove the pan from the heat, add the Gouda and bacon, and mix until incorporated. Pour the mixture into the prepared baking dish, cover with plastic wrap, and refrigerate for 3 hours, or until set.

When ready to fry the grits, preheat the oven to 200°F. Line a rimmed baking sheet with paper towels.

Whisk together the eggs and remaining 1 tablespoon water in a shallow dish. Put the panko in a separate shallow dish.

> **Stacy Lyn's Note**
> When you line the baking dish with parchment paper for the grits, allow the parchment to hang over all the sides. This will make removing and cutting the grits so much easier!

In a skillet, heat about 1 inch of vegetable oil over high heat to 350°F or until shimmering.

Cut the set grits into 9 square cakes. Dip each grits cake into the egg mixture, then dredge in the panko. Working in batches, gently place the cakes in the hot oil and fry for 2 to 3 minutes, until the panko turns golden. Turn the grits cakes over and cook for another 2 to 3 minutes, until they are warmed through and golden on the other side. Transfer to the prepared baking sheet. Keep warm in the oven while preparing the shrimp.

To make the shrimp, heat a griddle pan or cast iron skillet over high heat. Working in batches, place the shrimp about 1 inch apart in the pan and sprinkle with the salt and pepper from a height to distribute evenly. Cook for about 2 minutes, then turn the shrimp over and cook for another 1 minute, or until just cooked through. Transfer to a large bowl.

In a large nonstick skillet, heat the oil over medium-high heat until shimmering. Add the bell pepper, onion, celery, and garlic and sauté for 5 to 7 minutes, until softened, translucent, and starting to brown. Add the vinegars, soy sauce, and mustard and stir to incorporate. Cook for another 2 to 3 minutes, until the mixture thickens a little. Remove from the heat.

To make the aioli, heat a small skillet over high heat until smoking hot. Place the jalapeño in the skillet and cover with a lid to create a roasting effect. Flip the pepper every minute or so until all sides are charred evenly, about 8 minutes total. Remove the stem and skin from the pepper. Put the pepper in a food processor, add the mayonnaise, garlic, lemon juice, and salt, and blend until smooth. Check for seasoning.

To serve, put a grits cake on each plate. Add at least 4 shrimp, then top with the vegetable mixture, chopped bacon, and green onion. Drizzle with aioli and sprinkle with Parmigiano-Reggiano cheese.

FRIED CHEDDAR JALAPEÑO BALLS

❧ *Serves 12–14* ❧

8 ounces cream cheese, softened

2 cups shredded cheddar cheese

¼ cup chopped pickled jalapeños

¼ cup chopped cooked bacon

3 tablespoons Tabasco or other hot sauce

Peanut or vegetable oil, for frying

½ cup all-purpose flour

2 large eggs

1 tablespoon water

1 cup panko breadcrumbs

½ cup plain breadcrumbs

1 teaspoon onion powder

1 teaspoon garlic powder

½ teaspoon cayenne pepper

Kosher salt, for seasoning

¼ cup chopped fresh chives, basil leaves, and parsley

Line a rimmed baking sheet with parchment paper.

In a medium bowl, stir together the cream cheese, cheddar, pickled jalapeños, bacon, and hot sauce until well mixed.

Scoop about 2-tablespoon portions of the mixture to form 2-inch balls and place on the prepared baking sheet. Freeze the cheese balls for at least 30 minutes.

> **Stacy Lyn's Note**
> I like La Costeña pickled jalapeños. You'll find them in the olive aisle of the grocery store.

Fill a Dutch oven half full of oil and heat over medium-high heat to 375°F. Place a wire rack over a rimmed baking sheet.

Put the flour in a shallow dish. In a second shallow bowl, beat the eggs and water. In a third shallow dish, mix both breadcrumbs, the onion powder, garlic powder, and cayenne.

Working in batches, dredge the cheese balls first in the flour and then into the egg, then fully coat with the breadcrumbs.

Working in batches, carefully lower a few cheese balls into the oil and fry for about 3 minutes, until golden brown. Using a slotted spoon, transfer the cheese balls to the wire rack and allow to cool for 2 minutes. Sprinkle liberally with salt. Garnish with chives, basil, and parsley. Serve immediately.

Meat and Three

I don't know when it came on the scene, but we Southerners have been serving meat and three for as long as I've been around. If you aren't familiar with the term, it simply means a meat and three vegetables. And yes, mac and cheese counts as one of the vegetables!

If you asked any Southerner to say one word that comes to mind when they think meat and three, most of us would say *comfort*. Comfort is of utmost importance in the Southern home, and this Southern plate is a big part of that. It represents comfort for the soul and body.

waiting for him. I'd go over to her house during lunch to see them both. When Dad walked into her home and smelled the chicken frying and peas simmering, it was like the weight of the world fell off his shoulders. Of course, Granny's conversation was comfort to him, but this welcoming, seasonal friend of food was also a necessary ingredient.

The homestyle meat and three could have easily disappeared through the years, but it hasn't. It's the foundational Southern meal, and I believe it always will be. During the early twentieth century, as the would-be farmers came

The only thing more comforting than a meat and three is a meat and twelve shared with the ones you love.

In the South, many of us grew up eating at Grandma's house. Many of our grandmothers cooked what was in season from the backyard garden or nearest farmers' market. Along with a meat choice, usually fried or slow-cooked, seasonal vegetables round out the plate of endless comfort. By adding a bit of seasoning, including bacon grease, salt, and pepper, and topping with a little cheese or buttered crackers, the vegetables were transformed into a lifelong friend during happiness, stress, and even sadness in the life of a Southerner.

I think that's one of the reasons my dad ate at Granny's every single day he worked in town. He lived about forty minutes out of town, and Granny always had comfort on the plate

to the city in search of better job opportunities, they'd find a restaurant that served a meat and three–style meal like they were used to getting at home. Still today, businessmen and -women daily trek to one of my local favorite meat-and-three restaurants: Martin's.

Martin's has been a fixture in Montgomery since the 1930s. You can smell the chicken frying as you walk across the parking lot toward the corner of the strip mall. Its casual atmosphere makes it perfect for lawyers, students, politicians, and salespeople.

Not only is it the perfect place to conduct business, but it's also the perfect place for Sunday lunch on those days the dinner cook is not up for the task. And it happens—there

are weeks that Sunday sneaks up so fast, it will bite you! But since every Southerner knows Sunday dinner must not be canceled for any occasion, we also know the next best thing to a homemade meat-and-three meal at home is having it at a homey restaurant.

"Hey y'all. How many?" are the first words you hear upon entering Martin's, along with chairs scraping and happy voices. I often hesitate to answer the greeter's question because seating our family of nine can be a problem. We've gotten all kinds of reactions from startled laughter to "Don't you know what causes that?"

Soon enough we'll be seated, but in the meantime, I can't help but look at the plates full of food, hoping I'll be able to choose a meat and *only* three vegetables. I see hamburger steak with mushroom gravy. Crispy onion rings. Crumbly cornbread. Squash casserole. Creamed corn. Crispy fried chicken. Lima beans. Fried green tomatoes . . . all the meat-and-three classics.

How in the world can a person choose? Luckily Scott and I came up with a plan long ago that we still stick to: we share. Divide and conquer the menu, we call it. Over the last few years, when we go to Martin's, I've noticed the kids doing the same thing! The only thing more comforting than a meat and three is a meat and twelve shared with the ones you love.

HAMBURGER STEAK with MUSHROOM GRAVY

✑ *Serves 6* ✑

FOR THE PATTIES

2 pounds ground chuck

⅓ cup breadcrumbs

½ Vidalia or other sweet onion, finely minced

3 tablespoons Worcestershire sauce

1 tablespoon ketchup

1 teaspoon kosher salt

1 teaspoon freshly ground black pepper

1 teaspoon garlic powder

2 teaspoons chopped fresh thyme

2 tablespoons vegetable oil

FOR THE MUSHROOM GRAVY

2 tablespoons unsalted butter

12 ounces white button and/or cremini mushrooms, sliced

1 garlic clove, minced

3 tablespoons all-purpose flour

1½ cups beef stock

1 tablespoon Worcestershire sauce

Crispy Fried Onion Rings (page 29), for serving

Cooked long-grain white rice or mashed potatoes, for serving

To make the patties, combine the ground chuck, breadcrumbs, onion, Worcestershire, ketchup, salt, pepper, garlic powder, and thyme in a large bowl and gently mix until incorporated. Divide the meat mixture into six equal portions and shape into patties.

Heat the oil in a cast iron skillet over medium heat until shimmering. Working in batches, add the meat patties and cook for 4 to 5 minutes per side, until browned (the patties will not be cooked through). Transfer the patties to a plate and tent with aluminum foil.

To make the gravy, add the butter to the same skillet and allow to completely melt over medium heat. Add the sliced mushrooms and sauté for 5 to 6 minutes, until tender and golden. Add the garlic and cook for another 30 seconds. Add the flour and stir with a wooden spoon for about 2 minutes, until the flour is well incorporated into the mushrooms. Slowly add the stock to the skillet and whisk until the gravy is smooth. Stir in the Worcestershire sauce.

Reduce the heat to medium-low and add the partially cooked hamburger patties to the pan. Cook for about 7 minutes, flipping once, until the patties are cooked through. Top the patties with Crispy Fried Onions and serve over rice or mashed potatoes, fried green tomatoes, red heirloom tomatoes, and squash casserole.

CRISPY FRIED ONION RINGS

❧ *Serves 6* ❧

2½ cups buttermilk

2 tablespoons Tabasco or other hot sauce

2 large Vidalia onions, very thinly sliced

2½ cups all-purpose flour

1 tablespoon kosher salt, plus more for sprinkling

1 teaspoon freshly ground black pepper

Vegetable oil, for frying

In a large bowl, whisk together the buttermilk and hot sauce. Add the onions and stir until completely submerged.

In a separate large bowl, combine the flour, salt, and pepper.

In a Dutch oven, heat 4 inches of oil over high heat to 375°F. Set a wire rack in a rimmed baking sheet.

> **Stacy Lyn's Note**
> Crispy fried onions are perfect on burgers, alongside fried fish, and especially over steaks.

Working in batches, remove the onions from the buttermilk mixture and dredge in the flour mixture until completely coated, shaking off any excess flour. With a spider or slotted spoon, slowly lower the onions into the hot oil. Cook for about 2 minutes, until golden. If the onions bunch up, break them apart with the slotted spoon. Transfer the onions to the paper towels to drain. Sprinkle with extra salt and serve hot.

SQUASH CASSEROLE
∾ *Serves 10–12* ∾

6 yellow squash, sliced

1 large Vidalia or other sweet onion, coarsely chopped

2 large eggs

1 cup grated sharp cheddar cheese

1 cup grated Parmigiano-Reggiano cheese

1½ cups half-and-half or milk

1 teaspoon kosher salt

½ teaspoon freshly ground black pepper

¼ teaspoon cayenne pepper

2 sleeves butter crackers, such as Ritz

6 tablespoons unsalted butter, melted

Preheat the oven to 350°F. Coat a 3-quart casserole dish with cooking spray.

Bring a large stockpot of water to a boil. Add the squash and onion and cook over medium heat until tender, about 5 minutes. Drain well and set aside.

Meanwhile, in a medium bowl, lightly whisk the eggs. Add the cheeses, half-and-half, salt, black pepper, and cayenne pepper to the bowl and stir until combined. Mix the drained squash mixture into the egg mixture, then pour the combined mixture into the baking dish.

Roughly crush the crackers into a separate medium bowl. Add the melted butter and stir until all the crackers are coated. Spread the cracker mixture evenly on top of the casserole. Bake for about 40 minutes, until warm and bubbly around the edges and lightly toasted on top.

Stacy Lyn's Note
Store leftover fried green tomatoes in the refrigerator and reheat in a 200°F oven until warmed through, about 8 minutes.

FRIED GREEN TOMATOES
⟋ *Serves 10* ⟍

1 cup all-purpose flour

1 teaspoon kosher salt, plus
    more for sprinkling

½ teaspoon freshly ground
    black pepper

2 large eggs

1 tablespoon water

1 cup panko breadcrumbs

4 large, firm green tomatoes,
    sliced ¼ inch thick

1 cup vegetable oil

4 tablespoons (½ stick)
    unsalted butter

Place a wire rack over a rimmed baking sheet. In a large, shallow dish, mix the flour, salt, and pepper. In a second shallow dish, beat the eggs and water together. Put the panko in a third shallow dish. Coat the tomato slices first in the seasoned flour, then in the egg mixture, and finally in the breadcrumbs, and place on the wire rack.

Heat the oil and butter in a skillet over medium-high heat until sizzling. Working in batches, add the tomato slices and cook for 2 to 3 minutes per side, until golden and tender. Remove the slices to the wire rack while the remaining tomatoes are being cooked. Transfer to a platter, sprinkle with extra salt, and serve warm.

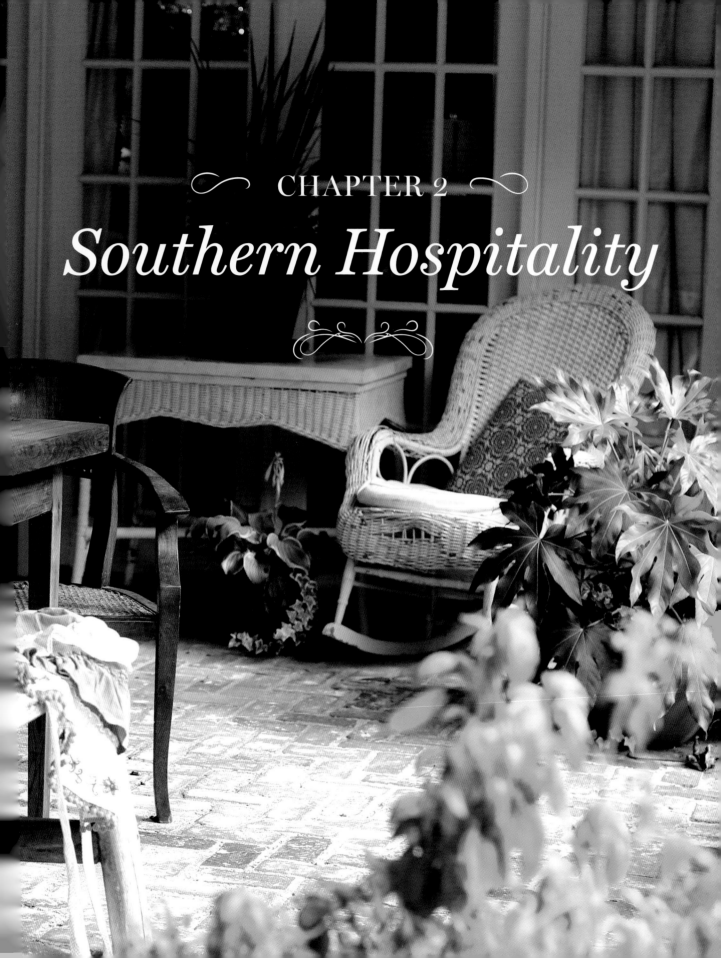

CHAPTER 2

Southern Hospitality

Southerners are bred to be hospitable. Basically from birth, Southern girls are taught charm and manners, and Southern boys are taught to be gentlemen. Becky had best be adorning a smile, even if her shoes are giving her a blister. Johnny must give up his seat if a lady enters the room and there are no seats left, even if he had to wake up early that morning and is bone tired. Nothing less will be tolerated.

Going the extra mile to make others feel comfortable, welcome, and appreciated, or to show compassion, is of utmost importance. A night, Scott and my mother-in-law, Kay, were explaining the rules of pickleball to me. Kay told me, "Sue is a champion at pickleball." And with the same breath and in the same sentence she concluded, "And did you know she makes the most amazing crust for her apple pie? You should get her to make it for you."

As you can see, although Sue is a champion of pickleball, her *true Southern identity* rests in the fact that she makes great crust! If I didn't live in the South, I may wonder, "What does Sue's crust have to do with pickleball?" Yet this all makes sense to a Southerner!

Putting others' needs above your own is at the heart of hospitality, and nine times out of ten, sweet tea, a slice of homemade cake, or a warm meal is hospitality's accompaniment.

handwritten card, a hostess gift always in hand, a homemade casserole, or merely an offer of sweet tea are all gestures of a heart of warmth and kindness taught by Southern parents. Putting others' needs above your own is at the heart of hospitality. These acts are merely the manifestation of the values ingrained into the hearts of Southerners.

Because food speaks of hospitality and love to Southerners, we become pretty good at making certain dishes, and they tend to identify us. Come to think of it, just last Hospitality is so ingrained in the Southerner that you will rarely find one of us without a tangible arsenal to pull from when we're in a pinch. When Angie's baby is born, or Mr. Taylor's dad passes, the Southerner will be ready to pull a casserole or cake from the freezer or put her apron on to get to fixin'! When the unannounced guest shows up at the door, there's always sweet tea, a warm cookie, or warm pound cake with melted butter, or if it is mealtime, a hot supper waiting to be lingered over at the table. That's the way of the South.

The Southerner's Arsenal

The *Oxford English Dictionary* defines *arsenal* as "an array of resources available for a certain purpose." Well, the Southern pantry, refrigerator, and freezer are always full of *resources* like sweet tea, icebox cookies, cakes, and casseroles ready for the *purpose* of at-the-drop-of-a-hat gracious hospitality. The Southern arsenal is consistently evaluated, improved upon, and truly central to the Southern home.

The fact is people drop by. And when they drop by, they come to the side door, just like family.

Slowly but surely, I've learned to take it as a compliment that folks come to the side door. That means they feel like family—no pretense, informal, and honest. Anyway, when friends see the worst of it, things can only get better!

Whichever door my guests use to enter, as soon as they are inside the arsenal opens. The first words that roll off my lips are, "Would you like some tea?" Whether they say yes or no, they will get tea, or a drink of some kind, along with whatever I can warm and serve in a moment's notice. Icebox cookies are always front and center in the freezer, and they take only ten

The side door represents real life, truth, family, no pretense. Sweet tea, cookies, and cakes are only the extension of the Southerner's gracious side-door heart.

Over the years, I've often found myself wondering: *Why can't you just use the front door?* The front porch has freshly watered ferns and flowers in pots and baskets, floor bricks swept and tidy, arrangements on the tables, and a welcome mat adorned with my house cat sprawled out like a king summoning guests to the double-paneled wooden doors and beyond into a clean, furniture-flanked foyer. The side entrance, on the other hand, is often a horror, with overgrown shrubs and boxes to be burned laid right outside the door, which opens straight into the heart of my house, the kitchen. It's never neat because it's always in use.

minutes to bake and serve on the Monticello reproduction china Scott gave me one year for my birthday. Sure, any plates will do, but it's a fun surprise and makes my guests feel special.

While the cookies are baking, I may flavor the sweet tea with peaches, berries, or whatever is in season, going the extra mile in making sure my guests have the best. It's always sweet tea, though, because sweet tea is to a Southerner what water is to a fish! It's the necessity of Southern life and hospitality. Refreshing. Life-giving. A visit just wouldn't be the same without it. Let's raise our glasses to friends who come through the side door like family and arsenals that are always ready to be unloaded for the ones we love.

SWEET ICED TEA
❧ *Serves 16 (1 gallon)* ❧

4 family-size tea bags

1½ cups sugar

Pinch baking soda

Lemon slices, for garnish

In a medium saucepan, bring about 1 quart water to a boil over medium heat. As soon as the water comes to a boil, immediately remove the saucepan from the heat. Add the tea bags and let the tea steep for 20 minutes. With a slotted spoon, remove the tea bags.

Put the sugar in a gallon-size pitcher. Pour about half of the hot tea into the pitcher and stir until the sugar is dissolved. Pour the remaining tea into the pitcher and stir. Add the baking soda and cold water to fill the pitcher and stir. Serve over ice with slices of lemon.

> **Stacy Lyn's Notes**
> I have a few important notes that every Southerner should know about making iced tea. Make sure you turn the heat off right when the water begins to boil. If you allow it to boil, it will become bitter. The pinch of baking soda will prevent the tea from becoming cloudy. Last but not least, Red Diamond is my family's favorite brand of tea, hands down.

WATERMELON LEMONADE
Serves 8

½ cup sugar

6 cups cold water, divided

4 cups watermelon cubes

Juice of 3 lemons

8 mint sprigs, for garnish (optional)

Make a simple syrup by combining the sugar and ½ cup of the water in a small saucepan. Bring to a boil, remove from the heat, and set aside to cool completely.

In a blender, blend the watermelon until smooth. Strain the watermelon puree through a fine-mesh strainer into a 2-quart pitcher. Add the syrup and lemon juice and stir to incorporate. Add the remaining 5½ cups water and top off with ice. Serve garnished with mint, if you like, and watermelon wedges, if you have leftover watermelon.

Stacy Lyn's Note
Although I think watermelon lemonade goes with just about anything, it's especially delicious on a hot summer day with hummingbird cake (page 58). Both are to die for!

PEACH TEA

◌ *Serves 8* ◌

4 large peaches, peeled, pitted, and sliced, or 4 cups frozen peach slices

2 cups water, plus more if needed

2 cups sugar

4 cups Sweet Iced Tea (page 40)

Mint sprigs, for garnish (optional)

In a large saucepan, bring the peaches, water, and sugar to a boil over medium-high heat. Cover, turn the heat down, and simmer until the peaches are soft, about 15 minutes. Mash the peaches to extract more flavor and cook for about 10 minutes longer.

Strain the peach mixture through a fine-mesh strainer into a gallon-size pitcher, pressing the peaches with the back of a spoon to extract as much juice as possible. Discard all that's left in the strainer.

Add the sweet iced tea to the pitcher and stir. Taste the tea. If the tea is too sweet or too strong, add additional cold water, 1 cup at a time, to your liking. Refrigerate the tea for at least 1 hour before serving. Stir well, then pour the tea over ice. Garnish with mint if desired.

Stacy Lyn's Note
My pet peeve is when tea gets watery as soon as the ice melts. So I like to use half ice and half frozen berries to keep the tea cold. That way, even on warm summer afternoons, the tea stays refreshing as long as the conversation lasts.

MIXED BERRY ICED TEA

❧ *Serves 8* ❧

3 cups mixed fresh or frozen berries, such as raspberries, blackberries, and blueberries, plus more for garnish

4 cups water

1½ cups sugar

4 cups Sweet Iced Tea (page 40)

2 lemons or limes, cut into rounds for the pitcher or wedges for the glasses, for garnish

Mint sprigs, for garnish (optional)

In a large saucepan, bring the berries, water, and sugar to a boil over medium-high heat. Turn the heat down and simmer uncovered for about 10 minutes, stirring occasionally. Pour the berry mixture through a fine-mesh strainer into a gallon-size pitcher, pressing the berries with the back of a spoon to squeeze out every last drop of juice. Discard all that's left in the strainer.

Add the iced tea to the pitcher and stir. Refrigerate the tea for at least 1 hour before serving. Add additional berries and lemon rounds to the pitcher, then pour over ice. Garnish with a wedge of lemon, a few berries, and a mint sprig, if desired.

KITCHEN SINK ICEBOX COOKIES

⟋ *Makes 3 dozen cookies* ⟍

2½ cups all-purpose flour

1¼ teaspoons baking soda

1 teaspoon kosher salt

1 cup (2 sticks) unsalted butter, softened

1¾ cups light brown sugar, firmly packed

1 tablespoon vanilla extract

1 large egg plus 1 large egg yolk

1 tablespoon warm water

1 pound dark chocolate, such as Lindt or Ghirardelli, chopped (about 2 cups)

½ cup semisweet chocolate chips

1½ cups crushed pretzels

1 cup toffee bits

Sea salt, for sprinkling

Preheat the oven to 350°F. Line three rimmed baking sheets with parchment paper.

In a medium bowl, whisk together the flour, baking soda, and kosher salt; set aside.

In the bowl of a stand mixer fitted with the paddle attachment, beat the butter on medium speed until creamy, about 3 minutes. Add the brown sugar and beat until the mixture is light and fluffy, about 4 minutes. Add the vanilla, egg and egg yolk, and warm water and mix on low speed until combined. Add the flour mixture and mix until combined. Add the chocolates, crushed pretzels, and toffee bits and mix until combined.

Drop rounded tablespoons of the dough on the prepared baking sheets, placing them about 2 inches apart. Freeze the dough on the baking sheets for 20 minutes. If you want to freeze the dough to bake later, leave it in the freezer for 12 hours, then transfer the cookies to a zip-top bag and store in the freezer until you are ready to bake them.

Sprinkle the cookies with sea salt. Bake for 10 minutes, or until the edges of the cookies are golden brown and the centers are set. Allow the cookies to cool for 3 minutes, then remove them to a wire rack to cool completely.

Stacy Lyn's Notes

To prepare the dough ahead of time to freeze, divide it in half. Lightly flour your hands and shape each half into a 1½- to 2-inch diameter log. Wrap each log in plastic wrap, then in freezer paper. They will keep in the freezer for up to 1 year. When you are ready to bake the cookies, preheat the oven to 350°F, then slice the log with a very sharp knife into ¼-inch-thick slices. Transfer them to a parchment-lined baking sheet, spacing them at least 2 inches apart, and bake for 10 to 12 minutes, until the edges are golden brown and the centers are set.

These are my all-time favorite cookies. They have everything—the sweet, the salty, and the crunchy. Absolute perfection!

Compassion in a Casserole . . . or Cake Pan

"Stacy, I just can't go through with this. Where are you? What are you doing?" were the words I heard on the phone line from my granny's hospital bed. She had been put in the hospital for a few tests and had been worried sick about it for days. She was frantic.

I dropped everything, got the kids settled, and headed to the hospital just as fast as I could. I only had five kids at the time and just discovered that week I was pregnant with number six, so I was battling morning sickness on top of wanting to care for Granny. I hadn't told anyone I was pregnant yet. Granny was one of eight and didn't like me having so many children because her mom had died during childbirth; her life was forever changed.

Dad in jeans, T-shirt, and a ballcap was just who I needed to see as I entered the hospital lobby. "Your granny has just been wheeled to the emergency room for a tracheotomy," Dad said solemnly. I'd noticed her having trouble breathing the past few times I'd talked to her, but thought she was just panicky. She had had a heart attack that morning.

It was hard to wrap my mind around the news. All I knew was that I wanted to see her.

She remained in ICU for a while but then was moved to a private room. A few days later, she was moved to long-term care, where I was convinced she would fully recover and be better than new. Dad and I walked toward her new room and met the doctor, who let us know that things were still serious. I felt like he gave us hope, but when I relayed everything he'd said to my mom, she said, "Stacy, do you hear what

you are saying?" "Of course, I do, Mom. What do you mean?" She continued, "I don't think the doctor is giving you hope at all."

Granny's room was quiet and bright. A cheery space with sun cascading brightly through the sheer curtains, giving a glow to the whitewashed walls. "Granny, do you want a little water?" Holding the straw up to her weak, parched lips, I smiled and said, "You're the best Granny in the world, and even in this bed, you are beautiful."

It seemed the entire day her eyes were fixed between Dad and me. It was obvious that her mind was perfectly alert, so Dad and I talked and reminisced about old times. I talked about the kids, plans we were making, and even about baby number six. Why not? I'd always shared everything with her.

All the while, nurses were coming and going, offering us drinks and snacks, and meeting our needs as well as Granny's. They'd fluff pillows, bring new drinks for Granny, and see to it that she was as comfortable as she could be.

Suddenly, it hit me like a brick between the eyes: They knew she was there to stay until her eyes met Jesus's, and they knew it was going to be soon.

I didn't want to leave her side but decided to go home to see the kids for an hour or so, then my plan was to come back and stay with Granny for the night. "Granny, I'm coming back within the hour. Try to get some rest." I had the eeriest feeling by the way she locked her eyes on mine that she knew it was the last time she would ever see me here on earth, but then I thought, "Nah, I'm just being paranoid." Sure enough, when I pulled into the driveway, Scott was on the porch talking on the phone, which he never does. Dad had just called and shared that Granny had passed after I left.

Disappointment and anger covered me like a blanket. I wanted to be with her when she went to glory. I believe to this day that she was just hanging on until I left. She was probably thinking, "When is she leaving? It is getting close." She did not want me there. I'm not sure small things you do, but they feel it. They leave refreshed, cared for, revived.

There's a reason *hospital* is the root word of *hospitality*. Hospitals are places where needs are met and treated, and illnesses are healed. We have the opportunity for this kind of hospitality more often than we think.

Young parents, you are showing hospitality every time you prepare dinner for your family. Grandparents, you, like my granny, are showing hospitality every time you look into the eyes of your grandchild and say, "Good job.

> Hospitality is much more than entertaining. It can also be simply, and sometimes invisibly, meeting the needs of others, whether in your home, through food shared, or just an attitude of acceptance. There's no pretense, no glory seeking, but merely meeting a need that refreshes, heals, revives, and comforts.

how I feel about that, but I know one day I'll be able to ask her why.

Looking back, it's interesting that I rarely noticed the nurses caring so greatly for our needs; they seemed to invisibly whisk in and out of the room without our noticing. Even though their jobs were to serve Granny and make her comfortable, they cared for our needs as well, always making us feel welcome and making sure we were also comfortable.

I've thought a lot about that day and how it changed my thoughts on the meaning of hospitality. Sure, there's an element of entertaining in hospitality, but authentic hospitality is invisibly meeting the needs of others, just like the nurses during our stay with Granny. The beneficiary may not notice all the

I love you," or make their favorite poppy seed casserole. You are bringing life, healing from the world's bullies, and nourishment to them.

Even without inviting folks into our homes, we can be hospitable by providing for them in their time of need.

Thankfully, I learned hospitality from the best. My granny didn't have much, but she had more love, attention, adoration, *and good eats* than I deserve. She healed me more than once. What a legacy she's left behind.

Granny, I can't wait to see you. Your face is one of the first I hope to see. I can't wait to sit at your table eating a piece of coconut cake, catching up, and hearing about your conversations with the saints that have been blessed to dine on your food. What a day that will be!

POPPY SEED CHICKEN

ᕙ *Serves 10–12* ᕚ

5 boneless, skinless chicken breasts

2 tablespoons olive oil

Kosher salt and freshly ground black pepper to taste

1 cup homemade or good-quality store-bought mayonnaise, such as Duke's or Hellmann's

1 (10.5-ounce) can cream of chicken soup

1 (16-ounce) container sour cream

1½ sleeves butter crackers, such as Ritz, crushed (about 2 cups)

12 tablespoons (1½ sticks) unsalted butter, melted

2 tablespoons poppy seeds

Cooked long-grain white rice, for serving

Preheat the oven to 425°F. Line a 9 x 13-inch baking dish with aluminum foil and lightly grease the foil.

Put the chicken breasts in a single layer in the prepared baking dish. Drizzle about half of the olive oil over the chicken and season with salt and pepper. Turn the breasts over and repeat. Bake for about 35 minutes, until they reach 165°F. Remove from the oven, shred the chicken using two forks, and set aside. Lower the oven temperature to 350°F and remove the foil from the baking dish.

In a large bowl, mix the mayonnaise, soup, and sour cream. Add the chicken to the mixture and gently stir until combined. Spoon the mixture into the baking dish.

In a medium bowl, combine the crushed crackers and melted butter and toss until all the crackers are coated with butter. Top the chicken mixture with the crackers and sprinkle the poppy seeds over the top of the crackers.

Bake for 25 to 30 minutes, until warmed through and bubbly. Serve hot over rice with a green salad and a squeeze of lemon.

> **Stacy Lyn's Note**
> If you're in a time crunch, use a 3-pound store-bought rotisserie chicken. Less stress for the cook wins every time in my book!

OLD-FASHIONED POUND CAKE

⟋ *Makes 2 loaves* ⟍

2¼ cups (4½ sticks) unsalted butter, softened

12 ounces cream cheese, softened

4½ cups sugar

1 tablespoon vanilla extract

1 tablespoon butter extract

Grated zest of ½ orange

9 large eggs, beaten

2¼ cups sifted all-purpose flour

2¼ cups sifted cake flour

1½ teaspoons kosher salt

Preheat the oven to 325°F. Butter and flour two 8½ x 4½-inch loaf pans.

In the bowl of a stand mixer fitted with the paddle attachment, beat the butter and cream cheese on high speed until creamy and blended, about 2 minutes. Slowly add the sugar and continue beating until light and fluffy, about 5 minutes. Add the vanilla and butter extracts and the orange zest and beat until incorporated. Slowly add the beaten eggs until incorporated.

In a medium bowl, mix the flours and salt. With the mixer on low, slowly add the flour until just mixed. Be careful not to overmix the batter as that will result in a tough, rubbery cake. Pour the batter evenly into the prepared pans.

Bake for about 1 hour 45 minutes, until the cakes are light and golden, a toothpick inserted in the middle of a cake comes out with loose crumbs, and the internal temperature of a cake reaches 200°F. Let the cakes cool in the pans for about 15 minutes, then remove the cakes from the pans and allow to cool completely on a wire rack.

> **Stacy Lyn's Note**
> If you are lucky enough to have leftover pound cake, wrap in plastic wrap and store at room temperature for up to 4 days to keep its freshness.

Life Is a Cakewalk . . . Sometimes

"I smell marijuana," I casually said to my stepdad, a retired green beret, as we walked through the fairgrounds. He snapped his head around to me in an instant, "What did you say?!" Not thinking anything at all about it, I said it again. "Where have you ever smelled marijuana? You don't even have your driver's license," he said with composure, but a touch of agitation.

I knew just where I'd smelled it: eight years earlier at the cakewalk, which at my elementary school was a version of musical chairs. They placed chairs in a circle and then the same number of kids, plus one, would

raised from the cakewalk event, and then told us that a policeman would begin walking down the aisles with lit marijuana, giving instruction to all the students to vacate any place where we may smell "this most unusual aroma."

I guess this exercise worked because I still remembered the smell eight years later, along with winning the cake that day. Mrs. Bibb let me keep my cake at her desk for safekeeping until the end of the day when I carefully carried it home. No one was home when I got there, and I just *had* to have a piece of the decadent chocolate cake—still my favorite to this day.

A cake is *always* appropriate. There is no occasion that a cake would not be welcomed! Talk about the symbol of perfect hospitality.

walk around the chairs as music played. Once the music stopped, each child would attempt to sit in the chairs as fast as possible, leaving one person without a chair. The last one to sit in the chair would win the cake! And yes, the effort is worth it! Cakes are always worth it.

Sure as the day is long, I won a cake! When the carnival was over, I grabbed my cake and took a seat with my class and Mrs. Bibb in the auditorium of my elementary school. Carefully placing my prize under my fold-up metal chair, I noticed a very strange smell. The principal took the stage, made a few announcements, sang the praises of how much money had been

Although the skunkish smell of marijuana and winning the decadent chocolate cake are seared into my memories of that day, my fondest recollection is that of all the proud parents bringing their cakes for the endless cakewalks, cake auctions, and cake contests. There were sheet cakes, tall round cakes, short round cakes, vanilla, strawberry, and some even loaded with candy. The kids were so proud of their parents for making the cakes, and there was a nostalgic air of happiness in the school that day.

I couldn't put it into words at such a young age, but what I was experiencing was charity—an

unselfish love for others. Those that had given of their time to make the cakes were beaming with joy, and it seemed to be contagious.

You see, in the South, cakes are love. The time and financial investment of making cakes for those you love are proof enough. Cakes say everything from "I hope you feel better" to "Happy Birthday." There's a cake for every occasion. And as my husband, Scott, says, "Cakes are always appropriate."

To me, for better or worse, marijuana and cakes are inseparably bound. (Well, they both do contain addictive qualities and change your mood and personality . . .) The school principal's message of that day was "Just say no" to the marijuana. I picked up on that, but I also learned a big "Just say yes" to cake! I'm sure my stepdad was thrilled on both counts, as we moved toward the annual cake bake-off tent to taste the best cakes in our city!

HUMMINGBIRD CAKE

❧ *Serves 15–18* ❧

FOR THE CAKE

2½ cups all-purpose flour

1 teaspoon baking soda

1 teaspoon ground cinnamon

½ teaspoon ground nutmeg

½ teaspoon kosher salt

1 cup light brown sugar, firmly packed

½ cup granulated sugar

3 large eggs

1 cup vegetable oil

1 teaspoon vanilla extract

1 (8-ounce) can crushed pineapple in juice

3 ripe bananas, mashed

2 cups pecans, toasted and finely chopped, divided

FOR THE FROSTING

12 ounces cream cheese, softened

¾ cup powdered sugar

3 cups heavy cream

1 teaspoon vanilla extract

Preheat the oven to 350°F. Lightly grease two 9-inch round cake pans and line the bottoms with parchment paper. Grease the parchment paper and dust the pans with flour, shaking out the excess flour.

In a medium bowl, whisk together flour, baking soda, cinnamon, nutmeg, and salt; set aside.

> ***Stacy Lyn's Note***
> The first time I tasted this recipe, I proclaimed, "This is the best cake I've ever tasted." This may be an exaggeration to some, but I stand by my statement.

To make the cake, in the bowl of a stand mixer fitted with the whisk attachment, beat the brown sugar, granulated sugar, and eggs on medium-high speed until creamy and light in color, 3 to 4 minutes. Slowly add the oil and vanilla and beat until incorporated. Using a spatula, fold in half of the flour mixture until combined. Add the pineapple with its juices and mashed bananas and fold until combined. Add the remaining flour mixture and fold until combined. Fold in 1 cup of the pecans.

Divide the batter evenly between the prepared cake pans and bake in the center of the oven for about 35 minutes, until the cakes are risen and springy to the touch and a toothpick inserted in the center comes out clean. Allow the cakes to cool in the pans for 5 minutes, then turn out onto a wire rack to cool completely.

While the cakes are cooling, make the frosting. In the stand mixer, whip the cream cheese and powdered sugar until completely combined, about 3 minutes. Add the cream and vanilla and whip until the frosting is light and fluffy.

When the cakes are cool, halve each cake horizontally to create four layers.

To assemble the cake, put one layer, bottom side up, on a serving platter and spread about ½ cup frosting evenly across the top. Top with a second cake layer, bottom side up, and add more frosting. Repeat with the next two layers, then spread the remaining frosting over the entire cake. Decorate the cake with the remaining 1½ cups pecans, or pipe small pineapples with colored icing on the tops and sides of the cake using a star tip. Refrigerate for 2 hours to allow the frosting to set before serving. This cake will keep in the refrigerator for up to 1 week or in the freezer for up to 1 month.

LANE CAKE
Serves 12–16

FOR THE CAKE

3¼ cups sifted cake flour

2 teaspoons baking powder

Pinch salt

1 cup (2 sticks) unsalted butter, softened

2 cups sugar

1 cup milk

1 teaspoon vanilla extract

8 large egg whites (reserve yolks for filling)

FOR THE FILLING

8 large egg yolks

1 cup sugar

8 tablespoons (1 stick) unsalted butter

1½ cups golden raisins, finely chopped

1 cup unsweetened shredded coconut

1 cup finely chopped pecans

3 tablespoons bourbon

1 teaspoon vanilla extract

FOR THE ICING

3 cups sugar

⅔ cup cold water

4 teaspoons light corn syrup

4 large egg whites

½ teaspoon cream of tartar

Pinch salt

Preheat the oven to 375°F. Butter and flour three 9-inch round cake pans.

To make the cake, in a medium bowl, whisk together the flour, baking powder, and salt; set aside.

In the bowl of a stand mixer fitted with the paddle attachment, cream the butter and sugar on high speed until light and fluffy. Add the flour mixture in three additions, alternating with the milk. Stir in the vanilla.

In a clean mixer bowl, using the whisk attachment, whisk the 8 egg whites on high speed until stiff. Gently fold the egg whites into the cake batter.

Divide the batter evenly into the prepared cake pans. Bake for 15 to 20 minutes, until the cakes spring back but have very little color on the top. Let the cakes cool in the pans on a wire rack for 15 minutes. Turn the cakes out onto the rack and allow them to cool completely.

Meanwhile, make the filling. In a small saucepan, whisk together the egg yolks, sugar, and butter over medium heat for about 20 minutes, until the mixture has thickened. Remove the pan from the heat and stir in the raisins, coconut, pecans, bourbon, and vanilla. Allow the mixture to cool.

(continued)

To make the icing, fill a saucepan with 2 inches of water and set a metal or heat-proof glass mixing bowl over the top, creating a double boiler. The bottom of the bowl should not touch the water. Bring the water to a boil over medium-high heat, then lower the heat to medium and continue to simmer. Add the sugar, water, corn syrup, egg whites, cream of tartar, and salt to the bowl. With an electric mixer, beat the egg whites until soft peaks form and the mixture is stiff and glossy, 10 to 15 minutes. Remove the bowl from the heat.

To assemble the cake, place one cake layer on a serving plate. Add half of the filling on top of the layer. Repeat with the second layer, then place the third layer on top. Cover the top and sides of the cake with the icing. If desired, decorate the top of the cake by lining the top edge and center with pecan halves. Store in the refrigerator for up to a week and in the freezer for up to a month.

Stacy Lyn's Notes

Lane cake is the official cake of Alabama, and rightly so, ever since Mrs. Emma Lane of Clayton, Alabama, entered her cake in the county fair. I have fond memories of my granny standing in her kitchen making her version of the Lane cake for birthdays and potlucks, or just for her family and friends. This is a perfect make-ahead recipe, as it tastes best 2 to 3 days after making it. If you have leftover icing, spread icing onto a parchment-lined baking sheet to about an inch thick and bake it at 200°F until it gets crunchy all the way through and serve with your favorite fruit.

CAPPUCCINO CAKE
❧ *Serves 15–18* ☙

FOR THE CAKE

2 cups buttermilk

1 cup vegetable oil

4 large eggs

1 tablespoon vanilla extract

2½ cups all-purpose flour

4 cups granulated sugar

1½ cups unsweetened cocoa powder, plus more for garnish (optional)

4 teaspoons baking soda

2 teaspoons baking powder

2 teaspoons kosher salt

2 cups freshly brewed hot coffee

FOR THE BUTTERCREAM FROSTING

1 cup (2 sticks) unsalted butter

3 cups powdered sugar

1 teaspoon vanilla extract

2 tablespoons heavy cream

FOR THE CAPPUCCINO FROSTING

3 ounces good milk chocolate, such as Ghirardelli or Callebaut, chopped

4 ounces good semisweet chocolate, such as Ghirardelli or Callebaut, chopped

1 cup (2 sticks) unsalted butter, room temperature

1½ cups powdered sugar

2 tablespoons very hot water

½ teaspoon espresso powder

2 tablespoons heavy cream

2 teaspoons vanilla extract

Fresh strawberries, for garnish (optional)

Preheat the oven to 350°F. Butter four 8-inch round cake pans and line the bottoms with parchment paper, then butter the parchment and flour the pans.

To make the cake, in a medium bowl, whisk together the buttermilk, oil, eggs, and vanilla; set aside.

Sift the flour, granulated sugar, cocoa powder, baking soda, baking powder, and salt into the bowl of a stand mixer fitted with the paddle attachment. Mix on low speed until combined. Slowly add the buttermilk mixture and mix until incorporated. Slowly add the coffee until just combined. Scrape down the sides and stir with the spatula until mixed well.

Pour the batter evenly into the prepared pans. Bake for 35 to 40 minutes, until a toothpick comes out clean. Allow the cakes to cool in the pans on a wire rack for about 10 minutes. Turn the cakes out onto the rack and let them cool completely.

Meanwhile, make the frostings. For the buttercream, in the bowl of a stand mixer fitted with the whisk attachment, mix the butter and sugar on low speed until incorporated, then on high speed until the mixture is light yellow and fluffy. Add the vanilla and heavy cream and beat for 3 minutes.

(continued)

To make the cappuccino frosting, fill a saucepan with 2 inches of water and set a metal or heat-proof glass bowl over the top, creating a double boiler. The bottom of the bowl should not touch the water. Bring the water to a boil over medium-high heat, then lower the heat to medium and continue to simmer. Add the milk and semisweet chocolates to the bowl and stir until just melted. Remove the bowl from the heat.

In the bowl of a stand mixer fitted with the whisk attachment, beat the butter on high speed until light yellow. Turn the speed down to low, gradually add the powdered sugar, and beat for 3 to 4 minutes, scraping down the sides of the bowl as needed.

In a small bowl, whisk together the hot water and espresso powder. Add the espresso mixture to the bowl of melted chocolate and mix until incorporated. With the mixer on low, slowly add the chocolate mixture, cream, and vanilla to the butter mixture and mix for 1 minute.

To assemble the cake, place one cake on a serving plate, bottom side up. Frost that layer with the buttercream. Repeat with the second and third layers and more buttercream. Place the fourth layer on top, bottom side up. Frost the top and sides of the cake with the cappuccino frosting. If desired, sift cocoa powder over the top of the cake and decorate with strawberries. Serve with vanilla or coffee ice cream, a few blackberries, and a sprig of mint for garnish.

> **Stacy Lyn's Note**
> Inevitably, I will have leftover icing. I like to fill a few pastry bags with various sized piping tips and decorate the edges and sides with the extra icing. Often I will make cupcakes for my family and top with the extra icing if I am saving the cake for a special occasion. When you make this cake, you really just can't wait to eat a slice!

CLASSIC COCONUT CAKE

❧ *Serves 12–14* ❧

FOR THE CAKE

4½ cups all-purpose flour

1 tablespoon baking powder

1½ teaspoons kosher salt

1½ cups (3 sticks) unsalted butter, softened

3 cups sugar

6 large eggs

1½ teaspoons vanilla extract

1½ cups whole milk (or the liquid from 2 fresh coconuts; add milk to the coconut liquid as needed to make 1½ cups)

FOR THE COCONUT ICING

4 cups sugar

2 cups water

8 large egg whites

8 cups sweetened shredded coconut or freshly grated coconut (from about 2 coconuts), divided

Vanilla ice cream, for serving (optional)

Preheat the oven to 350°F. Grease and flour four 9-inch round cake pans.

In a medium bowl, whisk together the flour, baking powder, and salt; set aside.

In the bowl of a stand mixer fitted with the whisk attachment, beat the butter on medium speed until creamy. Add the sugar and continue to beat, scraping down the sides as needed, until the mixture is light. One at a time, add the eggs, beating well until each one is incorporated and the batter is smooth and thick.

With the mixture on low speed, add one-third of the flour mixture and beat well until incorporated. Add the vanilla and half of the milk or coconut liquid and beat well. Grease and flour **three** 9-inch round cake pans. Continue beating as you add another third of the flour. Add the rest of the milk or coconut liquid and beat well. Add the remaining flour mixture and continue to beat until the batter is thick and smooth.

> **Stacy Lyn's Note**
>
> If you're using fresh coconuts, drill a few holes through the eyes of the coconut until you reach the hollow where the liquid is located (you can do this with a nail and hammer as well). Shake the coconut over a bowl until ½ to 1 cup liquid is drained out. With gentle force, tap the outside of the shell with a hammer until it cracks open. Separate the skin from the meat by placing a case knife or a spoon between the shell and the meat, as if you are shucking oysters. Once the shell is removed from the coconut, peel any excess flesh from the meat of the coconut.

Divide the batter evenly into the prepared pans and bake for 15 to 20 minutes, until the cakes are golden brown and begin to pull away from the sides of the pan. Let the cakes cool in their pans on a wire rack for about 10 minutes. Turn the cakes out onto the rack and let them cool completely.

Meanwhile, make the icing. In small saucepan, combine the sugar and water and bring to a boil over medium-high heat. Allow the mixture to cook over medium heat for about 3 minutes without stirring. Continue to boil for about 20 minutes more, stirring often, until the mixture has thickened and will form itself into threads about 2 inches long when poured from a spoon back into the pan. Set the mixture aside and let it cool.

In the bowl of a stand mixer fitted with the whisk attachment, whisk the egg whites on high speed until they are shiny, white, and full of volume. Pour the syrup slowly onto the edge of the bowl into the egg whites while beating at high speed until the egg whites and syrup are fully combined and create a fluffy white icing. This should take about 5 minutes, or until the bowl is room temperature. Fold in 4 cups of the shredded coconut. If the icing is too loose, place it in the refrigerator for about 10 minutes.

Once the cakes are cool, place one cake layer on a cake stand or serving plate and cover it with icing and a sprinkle of shredded coconut. Place the second layer on top of the iced layer, shaving any off the top to make it even. Spread another layer of icing over the top of the second layer and stabilize the cakes by lightly spreading icing around the sides. Add the last layer of the cake and spread icing over the top and evenly on the sides. Place the cake stand on a rimmed baking sheet and gently pat the sides with shredded coconut. Sprinkle the top of the cake with the remaining coconut. Serve alone or with a scoop of vanilla ice cream.

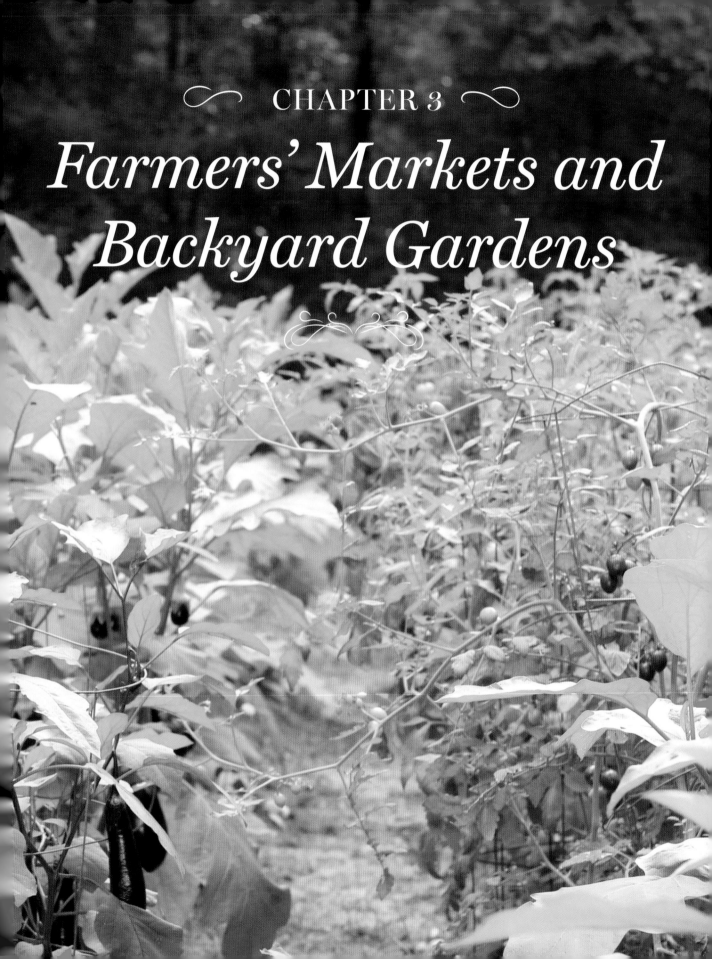

CHAPTER 3

Farmers' Markets and Backyard Gardens

Ah . . . the first days of summer. Sitting in the passenger seat of Granny's brownish-gold Oldsmobile, windows down since the air conditioning didn't work, early morning wind blowing through my hair. The whole way to the farmers' market I'd be anticipating drowning myself in peaches and cream, Granny's specialty. Of course, peaches and cream would have to wait until we'd meticulously looked over the rows and rows of tomatoes, squash, potatoes, plums, blueberries, strawberries, and vegetables and fruits I didn't even know existed!

We were headed for the coliseum parking lot, which doubled as a fairground in the fall. It always took circling around a few times to find just the right space, though we didn't mind the delay. Trucks from all over the county had come, and seeing how the people lined up helped whet our appetites—we were in for something good. Inside the market was booth after booth of farmers selling their hard-earned harvests. To regulars, like us, they would talk endlessly. And let me tell you, my Granny never heard a conversation she didn't want to join in on. I always knew it would be a long time before I finally got that big bowl of peaches and cream.

Granny was a gardener herself, but she couldn't grow everything she wanted in her own small kitchen garden. What she didn't grow, she bought from the locals who did. If she was waiting for her vegetables to ripen, she'd also buy from farmers who were a little ahead of her in the growing season. After shopping and talking and talking some more, she and I would finally make our way back to the Oldsmobile with arms burning from carrying the overloaded bags of veggies and fruits, and smiles on our faces, content as june bugs.

The morning dew would have evaporated by the time we returned home, so Granny and I would water the garden, pull a few weeds, and talk about what we would make with the bounty once it was ready. Once that work was done, we'd park ourselves just inside her screened door. That's where we'd spend the rest of the morning shelling peas and "looking them"—that is examining them for bugs. I tried hard not to mention the peaches I had been eyeing in the basket by the refrigerator. I was told not to beg, and by golly I was doing my darndest not to.

"Is it time for the peaches and cream, Granny?" I'd finally say in an adult voice, so as not to beg. Obviously, a little girl can only wait as long as she can wait. "Don't you think we should have lunch first?" she'd reply, with the same tone I'd asked. After tomato soup and a half grilled cheese, it was finally time for what I'd been waiting for. Paring knife in hand, Granny peeled the peaches like there was no tomorrow, and in a matter of minutes, the peach slices were floating in sweet milk sweetened with a little more sugar. By the way, "sweet milk" is whole milk—not to be confused with buttermilk. It's kind of strange,

Maybe the honor system isn't on every county road anymore, but that spirit is still alive in the South.

but previous generations differentiated whole milk and buttermilk by calling whole milk "sweet milk."

Granny's garden wasn't the only one in the family; my dad had a garden too. Huge and perfectly manicured, Dad's garden produced an exceptional bounty. I don't think he ever bought a single vegetable, unless the rabbits and deer mowed the vegetables down to nubs, and then he'd only buy them from the local farmers' market or nearby farms on the "honor system." I don't see this happening quite as much these days, but it used to be that farmers would place a stand on the roadside, where people could pull over, pick the produce they want, and put cash in a locked box for the farmer to retrieve later that night or in the morning. Whatever my dad produced in the garden or bought from the locals, he always shared with Granny, and she with him. That way, they both would get a little of everything.

Maybe the honor system isn't on every county road anymore, but that spirit is still alive in the South. Most of my neighbors grow a small garden, or at least a few vegetables in pots on the porch. We share garden bounty with each other and support the farmers' markets in the area. I think the markets will always be special to the people of the South—they are a place to meet with neighbors you haven't seen in a while, and a way to catch up on community news. In both rural areas and cities, farmers' markets dot what seems like every street not only because of Southern intuition that fresh ingredients create superior food, but because community is important to us. Sharing our garden vegetables, sharing stories from the week, and sharing our lives with one another, as well as supporting our local friends, tie social strings between us. And tying those strings is what the South is all about.

Hard Times, the Best of Times

A husband, wife, and three-month-old baby move to a strange city with no job and nowhere to live. "These will be the best years of your life," a kind lady, Eugenia, advised me. I wanted to believe her, but at the start there were moments I wasn't so sure.

These were what I referred to as our "Birmingham years." We had packed up our things, put our baby, Forrest, in the car seat in the back of the Trooper, and made our way to one of the smallest apartments I'd ever seen in a town where we knew virtually no one but where Scott would be attending dental school. We didn't have much, but we had big dreams and that's really all we needed, or so we thought as we pulled into our new adventure.

The engine on our Trooper blew soon after we arrived in Birmingham, leaving me vehicle-less for about eight months. Thankfully, the apartment we lived in was within walking distance of the grocery store, the laundromat (an adjustment for someone who was used to washing things right before I needed them), and what I would say is one of the loveliest botanical gardens in the world. As time went on, I learned to live in the tight quarters . . . in some ways I would say I learned to love them.

The kitchen was super tiny but prepared me to cook creatively using one dish—a skill that still serves me to this day! Since our backyard was shared with others, we had no privacy. For an outdoors introvert like

Scott, this was a challenge. To help him keep some semblance of normalcy, I prepared an enormous spread for the table each night while he continuously pored over the stacks of books that were starting to take over the little space we had.

We were living on next to nothing, so I got really good at cooking the basics. We ate *a lot* of red beans and rice—which by the way, we grew to love and keep on our rotation even today.

Every Sunday, we'd go hiking, Forrest in tow on one of our backs in our worn-out backpack, and afterwards grab a Blizzard from the nearest Dairy Queen, then drive around in the country. We were headed down a main

Yep. I ordered them before we even moved in. But that was the reason we wanted the house in the first place.

We harvested so many tomatoes that year, we could have set up our own farm stand out front. Summer panzanella had never tasted so good or been easier to make, with all the ingredients right in the backyard. We grew squash, peppers, eggplant, melons, tomatoes, peas. Canning was a regular evening event. Squash relish, chowchow, and canned tomatoes were given as Christmas gifts that year.

Our garden perfectly symbolized the newfound freedom we were experiencing. Simplicity. You plant a seed, water it, watch

Living with the basics and loving each other all the more is your best life.

street in a little town outside Birmingham when I noticed an open house situated on a huge lot—big enough for my dream garden. We stopped and toured with the other thousand prospective buyers.

It wasn't much bigger than a double-wide, but it felt like the Taj Mahal to me. I was sold. Scott said I could make an offer if the payments would be lower than the rent on our apartment, so I made a few calls and figured out a price to offer, which was much less than the asking price. They denied it, but my faith was strong that they would be calling me back. I prayed and waited.

Sure enough, the owners called and took our offer.

But first things first. What did I do as soon as I found out the house was ours? I ordered seeds.

it grow, protect it, and harvest it. The basics. We were living with the basics and loving each other all the more. Our lives would never be the same again. That's a good thing. We came back to our hometown very different people than we left. I couldn't be more thankful.

Freedom: that's the word that describes our years in Birmingham. Not only were we beginning to live off the land for our food, but we were also truly becoming independent from all we had known. We were on our own, becoming thinkers, making decisions that others may not like, but becoming exactly who we were supposed to be. Free from excess. Free from stuff. It was like breathing in fresh air for the first time.

Eugenia, you were right, those were some of the best years of my life. I've never learned so much as in those years.

AUTHENTIC RED BEANS AND RICE

❧ *Serves 14–16* ❧

2 pounds dried red beans

4 tablespoons vegetable oil,
    divided

1 pound andouille sausage
    or other smoked sausage,
    sliced ½ inch thick

2 Vidalia or other sweet onions,
    chopped

1 green bell pepper, seeded
    and chopped

4 celery stalks, chopped

4 garlic cloves, minced

1 tablespoon kosher salt

2 teaspoons Creole seasoning

2 teaspoons dried thyme

1 teaspoon cayenne pepper

1 teaspoon freshly ground
    black pepper

3 bay leaves

1 ham hock

3½–4 quarts chicken stock

1 bunch parsley, chopped
    (about 1 cup)

1 bunch green onions, thinly
    sliced (about 1 cup)

Cooked long-grain white rice,
    for serving

In a colander, rinse the beans under cool running water. Transfer the beans to a large
pot and add enough water to cover the beans by at least 1 inch. Soak for at least 4
hours or overnight. Drain.

In a Dutch oven, heat 1 tablespoon of the oil over medium-high heat. Add the sausage
and brown until slightly crisp, about 10 minutes.

Add the remaining 3 tablespoons oil, the onions, bell pepper, and celery, and cook
until the vegetables are translucent, about 4 minutes. Add the garlic and cook for
another minute. Stir in the salt, Creole seasoning, thyme, cayenne, and black pepper.
Add the bay leaves and ham hock and cook for 2 minutes.

Pour the drained beans into the pot and add enough stock to cover the beans by
at least 1 inch. Bring to a boil over high heat, then reduce the heat to medium-low.
Simmer for about 2 hours, stirring occasionally, until the beans are tender.

Remove and discard the bay leaves. Remove the ham hock, pull off any loose meat, and
return it to the beans. Transfer about 2 cups of the cooked beans to a small bowl and
mash the beans with a fork or use an immersion blender to thicken the beans and create
a creamy texture, then return the mashed beans to the pot. Add half of the parsley and
half of the green onions and stir until incorporated. Simmer for about 15 minutes. Taste
and adjust the seasoning and add water or stock if the beans are too thick.

Spoon the beans into bowls and top with rice. Garnish with the remaining parsley and
green onions and the lime wedges.

Stacy Lyn's Note

If you don't have time to soak the beans for at least 4 hours, rinse the beans, transfer them to a Dutch oven, and cover with at least 1 inch of water. Bring to a boil and cook for 3 minutes, then remove from the heat and cover. Let stand for 1 hour, then drain and proceed with the recipe.

GREEN TOMATO CHOWCHOW
❧ *Makes 4 pints* ❧

5 large green tomatoes, cored and diced

1 cup chopped green cabbage

1 Vidalia onion, diced

2 jalapeño peppers, seeded and finely chopped

1 green bell pepper, seeded and chopped

1 red bell pepper, seeded and chopped

4 celery stalks, chopped

½ teaspoon kosher salt

1 tablespoon mustard seeds

1½ teaspoons whole black peppercorns

½ teaspoon ground nutmeg

½ teaspoon ground turmeric

1 cup apple cider vinegar

2 cups distilled white vinegar

2 cups sugar

1 tablespoon Dijon mustard

2 teaspoons red pepper flakes

½ teaspoon ground ginger

In a large nonreactive bowl, mix the green tomatoes, cabbage, onion, jalapeños, bell peppers, celery, and salt. Cover and chill overnight. Transfer the vegetables to a colander and drain off any liquid that has accumulated.

In a Dutch oven, toast the mustard seeds, peppercorns, nutmeg, and turmeric over medium heat for about 1 minute, until fragrant, continuously moving the pot in a swirling motion to keep the spices from burning. Add both vinegars, the sugar, mustard, red pepper flakes, and ginger. Bring to a boil, then reduce to a simmer and allow the mixture to reduce for about 5 minutes. Turn off the heat and add the vegetable mixture to the pot; mix well. Let cool to room temperature.

Using a slotted spoon, divide the vegetables into four pint-size mason jars or other airtight containers, then fill each container evenly with the liquid from the pot. Store in the refrigerator for up to 1 week.

Stacy Lyn's Note
Mason jars are perfect for storing chowchow, and once you taste this green tomato chowchow, I just know you'll want to can as much as possible for the entire year. It's a perfect accompaniment to peas, beans, meats, and fish—you truly can't ever have too much! You can process the chowchow using the hot water bath canning method for long-term storage.

SQUASH RELISH

❧ *Makes 4 pints* ❧

4 pounds summer squash
(8 to 10 large squash),
seeded and shredded

3 jalapeño peppers, seeded
and diced

2 Vidalia or other sweet onions,
diced

Prepare four pint-size canning
jars for canning.

6 tablespoons canning salt

3¾ cups sugar

3 cups apple cider vinegar

1 tablespoon ground turmeric

1 tablespoon ground mustard

2 teaspoons celery seeds

½ teaspoon ground nutmeg

½ teaspoon cayenne pepper

In a large bowl, combine the squash, jalapeños, onions, and canning salt. Cover and refrigerate for 8 hours. Drain, rinse with cool water, and drain again. Pat the squash with paper towels, removing as much liquid as possible. Allow the squash to sit on several layers of paper towels for about 30 minutes, until much of the moisture is released.

In a large pot, combine the sugar, vinegar, turmeric, mustard, celery seeds, nutmeg, and cayenne and bring to a boil while gently stirring. Reduce the heat and simmer for about 20 minutes.

Gently ladle the mixture into the prepared jars, leaving ½ inch headspace. Wipe the rims clean, place the hot lids on the jars, and loosely screw on the bands. Process using the hot water bath canning method for 15 minutes. Place the jars on a kitchen towel and allow to come to room temperature.

If you have any extra relish, store in an airtight jar in the refrigerator and use within a week or two.

> **Stacy Lyn's Note**
> Squash relish is a perfect accompaniment all year long for peas, hot dogs, collards, hamburgers, or roasted lamb. Not only is it a delicious condiment, but it's healthy too. My mom says squash aids in vision, and I've heard it can help prevent insomnia! You can also process the relish using the pressure canning method for long-term storage.

ROASTED TOMATO SOUP WITH GRILLED CHEESE SANDWICH CROUTONS

❦ *Serves 4* ❧

FOR THE SOUP

3 pounds tomatoes, halved lengthwise

2 tablespoons unsalted butter

1 onion, chopped

2 carrots, chopped

1 cup vegetable stock

½ teaspoon chopped fresh basil, plus whole basil leaves for garnish

½ teaspoon chopped fresh oregano

⅓ cup heavy cream

Kosher salt and freshly ground black pepper to taste

FOR THE GRILLED CHEESE CROUTONS

4 (½-inch-thick) slices sourdough bread

4 tablespoons (½ stick) unsalted butter, melted

4 ounces cheddar cheese, grated

To start the soup, preheat the oven to 450°F. Line a rimmed baking sheet with parchment paper.

Place the tomatoes cut side down on the prepared baking sheet and roast for 12 minutes. Set aside until cool enough to handle, then remove and discard the skins.

Melt the butter in a heavy-bottomed stockpot over medium heat. Add the onion and carrots and cook until soft, about 8 to 10 minutes. Stir in the tomatoes, stock, basil, and oregano and bring to a boil. Lower the heat to a simmer, cover the pot, and simmer for 20 minutes.

Meanwhile, make the grilled cheese croutons. Heat a griddle pan or cast iron skillet over medium-high heat. Brush the pieces of bread on one side with the melted butter. Turn two pieces of bread over and scatter half of the cheese on each piece. Place the other two pieces of bread on top, buttered side up.

Grill the sandwiches on one side for about 3 minutes, until nicely browned, adding a weight or pressing the sandwiches down with a spatula while cooking. Turn the sandwiches over and cook for another 2 to 3 minutes, again pressing down, until the cheese is melted and the other side is nicely browned. Transfer the sandwiches to a cutting board and allow to rest for about 2 minutes. Cut each sandwich into 1-inch cubes and set aside until ready to serve.

Carefully transfer the tomato mixture to a food processor and puree. Return the soup to the pot and rewarm over medium heat. Turn off the heat and stir in the heavy cream. Season with salt and pepper. Ladle the soup into bowls and sprinkle the croutons on top.

Stacy Lyn's Note
This roasted tomato soup is perfect alone, but when you add the grilled cheese croutons, it goes to a whole new level. The croutons are also great served in Summer Panzanella (page 83)!

SUMMER PANZANELLA

◦ Serves 6–8 ◦

8 ripe but firm heirloom tomatoes, cored and cut into 2-inch chunks

1 ear corn, kernels cut from the cob

1 red onion, thinly sliced

4 garlic cloves, minced, divided

4 tablespoons balsamic vinegar, divided

2 tablespoons plus ¼ cup extra-virgin olive oil, divided, plus more for drizzling

2 tablespoons kosher salt, divided, plus more for seasoning

1 tablespoon freshly ground black pepper, divided, plus more for seasoning

Leaves from 1 bunch basil (about ½ cup), plus more for garnish

1 loaf crusty sourdough bread, torn into 2-inch chunks

Preheat the oven to 400°F.

In a large bowl, combine the tomatoes, corn, onion, half of the garlic, 2 tablespoons of the vinegar, 2 tablespoons of the olive oil, 1 tablespoon of the salt, and 1½ teaspoons of the pepper. Tear the basil leaves over the tomatoes, toss well, and set aside while you make the croutons.

Put the bread chunks in a medium bowl. Drizzle with the remaining ¼ cup olive oil and add the remaining garlic, remaining 1 tablespoon salt, and remaining 1½ teaspoons pepper. Toss the bread to evenly coat, then adjust the seasoning to your liking. Spread out the bread in a single layer on a rimmed baking sheet and bake until the croutons are golden brown, 10 to 12 minutes.

Transfer the croutons to a serving bowl. Pour the tomato mixture over the croutons and toss. Drizzle a little olive oil and the remaining 2 tablespoons vinegar over the top, add a few basil leaves, and serve immediately.

CHAPTER 4

Home Matters

illy creating handmade note cards at the bar watching the fresh vegetable soup on the stove. Anna poring over geometry at the long table in the dining room. Mary finishing up research for a project and then making a grocery list for next week. Howlett fixing the chicken coop to keep coyotes out. Graylyn putting on her boots to get eggs from the coop to make a cake for Mrs. Baker, who just lost her husband. Hampton painting the outside of the house that so desperately needs it. Me harvesting vegetables from the backyard garden to test a recipe and feed a hungry household. Pretty much, this is what you'd see, or something like it, if you were to drop by at any time during the day.

is where we connect, not just for holidays, but every day. Order, beauty, and peaceful surroundings define the Southern home to make the backdrop of relationships, creativity, and hospitality inviting and comfortable. I believe that's why the porch is central to the Southern home. With the outdoor surroundings and some comfortable seating, it draws people together. People long to be home and work to get there at all times of the day.

It's not unusual for the postman to drive up to the house during lunch while our entire family is spread out all over the porch devouring vegetable soup and grilled cheese, or mac and cheese, potato salad, fried chicken, and sweet tea. Come to think of it, just about

Beauty, order, and comfortable surroundings define the Southern home and create a backdrop where relationships, creativity, and hospitality can flourish.

This is home.

For the Southerner, life begins and ends at home. It's central in our hearts. It's where we invest our time, hope, and future. Instead of the world, jobs, or community life "out there" defining us and being our solace, home is our safe place and where industry begins, and creativity is sparked. The Southerner just can't wait to get home to recharge to invent ideas that will help the family or the world. We need to be home to relax enough for the creative energies to flow. Home is intimate and necessitates thought.

Home is also a beautiful landing ground for relationships to flourish. Our home base

any time of the day, whether winter, spring, summer, or fall, at least a few of us are on the porch studying, working, or just talking when the postman delivers the mail.

Scott's dad walked home every day from work for lunch. Scott comes home every day for lunch, and now, Forrest goes home for lunch when Becca isn't working. All the kids who have jobs or are in school come home for lunch at the same time as Scott, so that we can spend a few minutes together before the end of the day. You could call this *our* family tradition, but many Southern families meet at their homes to eat lunch together daily or

weekly. My dad went to his mom's house for lunch for over twenty years. It's just what we do. It keeps us close.

Southerners' homes reflect who we are, because we truly live, dream, create, and work in our homes. It's the place we display treasures from a lifetime of experiences. From the minute you walk into a Southerner's home, you can tell exactly what they believe, what's important to them, and who they are; it's quite vulnerable. We like it this way. We work to make it reflect ourselves. With a little loving care, even the humblest of homes becomes the most comfortable place on earth. It's a way of showing hospitality—inviting and serving someone from your world.

Since the home is a place of rest, celebration, hospitality, creativity, industry, healing, and blessing, our desire is to make it comfortable and beautiful. A necessity that facilitates the best parts of life. Home, sweet, Southern Home—it's what we're all about.

Unfortunate Events and a
PBS Special Change Our Course

"Mom, do you like my bathing suit for the beach?" four-year-old Graylyn asks as she parades down the hall toward me with kids' scissors in hand and her hair cut in a bob up to her ears. As I am having a mini stroke, her brother, two-and-a-half at the time, trails after her with his own new haircut, pretty much to the scalp. We'd just finished watching *The Parent Trap*, and apparently, they'd learned a few things!

Scott's great-great-grandfather owned land and several homes along the Mississippi River, which Scott had never seen. During his great-great-grandfather's life, he'd given a parcel of land to each of his children to build a home. Most were huge, but one home was quite modest and was, at one time, part of the Natchez Historic Homes. This property, Mistletoe Plantation, remained in Scott's family for over a hundred years until it was sold. Even

You never know when a change in plans can lead you around a wonderful corner in life. Staying open keeps us sane . . . and growing!

All set for our beach trip. Four kids packed and ready, and two sporting new haircuts, the phone rings with news that we'd mixed up the dates on the beach house and someone else was staying there. Scott had canceled patients, given the days off to his employees—and we were packed, which was a huge feat in itself. What a disappointment. I wanted to faint; yes, that's dramatic, but just saying.

"I have it! Let's go to Mississippi!" Scott said with jubilant excitement. I was like, "What? What are we going to do in Mississippi besides eat Mississippi mud cake? Though . . . I do love Mississippi mud cake." That's all it took for me. I'm game.

though we had no idea who lived in it now, we both had high hopes of being able to see it.

We spent a week in Mississippi walking parts of the Natchez Trace, touring historic homes, eating at the best restaurants we could find, and tasting every Mississippi mud cake we could get our hands on because I was going to make the best one to ever be made! On our last day in Natchez, with great anticipation, we drove to the homesite. Lo and behold, the gate was open! This was much to Scott's distress as he knew I would want to drive in . . . and be invited in. And that is exactly what I did. What's the worst that would happen—a little embarrassment? As it ended up, the gate was open because the owners were home. And upon explaining our relationship to the house, they were delighted to show us around.

We returned home with new friends and a new appreciation for history and historic homes. We'd just started watching a PBS series, *Frontier House,* a historic reality series where three family groups agree to live as 1883 homesteaders for five months in one-room cabins in Montana. In the series, a very affluent family of five, the parents and three kids, from Malibu, California, stood out to me. Before and after their time on the show, the kids admitted to being bored and unhappy though they seemingly had everything. During the show, about a month after being off-grid and in the trenches of homestead life, the kids were laughing as they worked, the parents were smiling and enjoying one another, and they had truly united as a family. It was genuine.

This got Scott and me thinking about our future home. We'd just had plans drawn for a Tudor-style home. It was planned to be pretty massive, with only a small porch on the back and large bedrooms. Scott and I decided to scratch that mansion-like house and create a home conducive to relationship building and industry. We wanted gardens to work, porches to sit, talk, and host friends and family, as well as a central place that we could congregate, like an open kitchen and den area.

It hit us. The house from Mississippi, Mistletoe Plantation, would meet all the requirements. It had it all. Front and back porches, a centralized area for congregating inside, and wings for the bedrooms. I wrote to the new owners of the family home thanking

them for their hospitality and telling them that we loved Mistletoe so much that we were going to replicate it. They kindly sent us dirt from the property and a few bricks to weave into the home. We placed the bricks in the hearth on the fireplaces and the dirt as we dug the foundation. Using that home as a blueprint has served us well. Our home has been a place of love, nurture, and industry. I wouldn't want to live anywhere else.

Disappointments may lead you right into the place you are meant to be. No, we didn't go to the beach on that trip, but a vacation to Mississippi instead, and a PBS show resulted in a beautiful life raising children in a most beautiful way. The Southern way.

GRANNY'S VEGETABLE SOUP . . . WITH BEEF

❧ *Serves 8–10* ❧

½ cup all-purpose flour

2 tablespoons kosher salt, divided

2 teaspoons freshly ground black pepper, divided

2 pounds beef chuck, cut into 2-inch cubes

4 tablespoons vegetable oil, divided

3 cups beef stock

2 celery stalks, finely chopped

1 large onion, finely chopped

1 garlic clove, minced

1 pound okra, sliced into ¼-inch-thick rounds

8–10 tomatoes, peeled and roughly chopped

¾ cup butter beans

4 ears light yellow corn, kernels cut off the cobs (about 1 cup)

1 tablespoon finely chopped fresh basil, plus more for garnish

1 tablespoon chopped fresh thyme, plus more for garnish

3 dashes Tabasco or other hot sauce

1 lemon, cut in half

Sour cream, for serving (optional)

Fried Jalapeño Cornbread (page 10), for serving

In a shallow bowl, whisk together the flour, 1 tablespoon of the salt, and 1 teaspoon of the pepper until well combined. Dredge the beef cubes in the seasoned flour, shaking any excess flour off.

In a Dutch oven, heat 2 tablespoons of the oil over medium-high heat until shimmering. Add half of the beef to the Dutch oven in a single layer and cook until browned, 2 to 3 minutes per side. Transfer the beef to a large bowl. Repeat with the remaining beef. Return all the beef to the Dutch oven, add the beef stock, and bring to a boil over high heat. Cover, lower the heat, and simmer for about 3 hours, until fork tender.

> ### Stacy Lyn's Note
> I love using a pressure cooker or Instant Pot to cook the beef for this recipe because it takes half the time to create succulent, tender meat and flavor. Heat the pressure cooker over medium-high heat. Working in batches, brown the floured meat on all sides in the cooker, then transfer to a large bowl. Return the beef to the pressure cooker. Add ¾ cup beef stock, 1 teaspoon kosher salt, and ½ teaspoon freshly ground black pepper and place the lid on the pot, sealing the pot according to the manufacturer's directions. Bring the pressure cooker up to full pressure over medium-high heat and cook for 15 to 20 minutes. You will hear the valve jiggling. Release the pressure according to the manufacturer's instructions. Test for fork tenderness, then transfer the beef and liquid to the soup. Simmer for 30 minutes.

Meanwhile, in a large stockpot, heat the remaining 2 tablespoons oil over medium heat. Add the celery and onion and cook for about 3 minutes. Add the garlic and cook for about 1 minute, stirring constantly. Add the okra, tomatoes, beans, corn, basil, thyme, hot sauce, remaining 1 tablespoon salt, and remaining 1 teaspoon pepper and stir well. Squeeze the lemon over the soup. Add just enough water to just submerge all the vegetables. Bring the mixture to a boil, then cover, lower the heat, and simmer for 30 minutes.

With a slotted spoon, remove the beef from the Dutch oven and add it to the soup. Simmer for another hour, adding a little stock if the soup gets dry. (Strain and freeze any leftover stock for future use.) Garnish with additional basil and thyme. Serve the soup with a dollop of sour cream (if using) and cornbread.

MISSISSIPPI MUD CAKE

❧ *Serves 12–14* ❧

1¼ cups buttermilk

¾ cup vegetable oil

2 large eggs

2 teaspoons vanilla extract, divided

2 cups all-purpose flour

1¼ cups granulated sugar

1 cup unsweetened cocoa powder, divided

2 teaspoons baking soda

1 teaspoon plus a pinch kosher salt

1 (10.5-ounce) bag mini marshmallows

1 cup (2 sticks) unsalted butter

¼ cup milk

1 pound powdered sugar (3½ cups)

1½ cups chopped pecans

Preheat the oven to 325°F. Grease and flour a 13 x 9-inch baking pan.

In a large bowl, whisk together the buttermilk, oil, eggs, and 1 teaspoon of the vanilla.

In a medium bowl, whisk together the flour, granulated sugar, ¾ cup of the cocoa powder, the baking soda, and 1 teaspoon of the salt. Pour the dry ingredients into the wet ingredients and mix until incorporated.

Pour the batter into the prepared pan. Bake for 20 minutes, or until a toothpick inserted into the center of the cake comes out with very moist crumbs. Do not overbake.

When the cake is done, sprinkle the marshmallows over the entire surface. Place the cake with the marshmallows back in the oven and bake until the marshmallows have melted, about 4 minutes. Allow the cake to cool for about 15 minutes.

While the cake is cooling, make the frosting. In a medium saucepan, combine the butter, milk, and remaining ¼ cup cocoa powder and heat over medium-low heat. Stir for 2 to 3 minutes, until all the ingredients have been incorporated and there are no lumps. Remove from the heat and whisk in the powdered sugar. Mix in the nuts, remaining 1 teaspoon vanilla, and remaining pinch of salt.

Pour the warm frosting over the cake. Allow the cake to cool before serving.

Stacy Lyn's Note
Since this cake goes back into the oven for about 4 minutes to brown the marshmallows, it is easy to overbake. You'll want to have moist crumbs on the toothpick when you check for doneness.

Little Cabin in the Woods

One thing that's true about marrying a visionary type of man: Life never gets boring. Since we were married, one of Scott's many visions has been building a cabin in the woods. When I say in the woods, I mean 100 percent off-grid at the foothills of the Appalachian Mountains. No electricity or water.

Plenty of times, mostly while considering spending time in a cabin with no electricity or water, I've asked myself what Scott's fascination with this vision might be. During the building process, I discovered the answer nowhere, if you know what I mean. It's nice just to make do with what you have, be content, and enjoy nature and each other without interruption. Don't get me wrong, I love the luxuries in today's world: electricity, hot water, television, and especially air conditioning (a huge priority for me here in Alabama).

So, building an off-grid log cabin was our answer.

At the time, we had five kids under ten years old, plus one on the way. Scott and the boys built out the loft, stairs, interior walls,

> Everyone needs a safe place to escape from the fast pace of the world and detox, even if it's just a rope swing in the backyard. If you don't have one, find one . . . *and fast*!

to that question. He had the same reasons for building the log cabin that the pioneers had before him: they knew there was something better out there. The hardship was worth it for the pioneers to find what they were looking for. Subconsciously, I believe Scott was also longing for what the pioneers had in family life: adventure, independence, and a simple life. I don't mean easier, just simpler.

When our kids were all young, we realized that we needed a way to escape the rat race. There is something appealing about escaping today's fast-paced world, including technology. Sometimes you just need to detox—get away from running here and there but getting porches, and windows, put in the electrical lines, plumbing lines, and gas lines, and then laid the floors. A septic system was a must, so that went in as well. We all took part in chinking the outside and inside of the cabin. I remember sweating bullets while chinking the logs in the hot sun in my humongous state, many months along in my pregnancy while trying to keep Graylyn from making fingerprints polka dots throughout. After all that, it was time to bring in the kitchen! We bought a propane-powered stove, refrigerator, oven, and lights. We added a generator for additional power for the air conditioning. Solar panels were used to

charge the battery for the generator. Voilà! By George, we had a cabin. The stories those walls could tell.

Of course, we played a lot in between building the cabin. There was a huge creek leading to a river on that land that we swam in and brought crawfish and fish back to the cabin to cook. Our favorite: crawfish mac and cheese! We hiked, foraged, and rode bikes. Hunting season brought even more adventures and food for the family. Everyone felt they had contributed to the welfare of everyone else, so being rewarded with fun times and good food was all the sweeter.

Escaping to our paradise was salvation in many ways. Having such a large family and adding to its number every two years makes for a very full and busy life. Scott and I chose to go against the grain a bit and said no to many great things. We limited the kids' individual activities to make space for those we could do as a family and with friends out in the open air, woods, and water.

I can't say that it wasn't hard, and that I loved every minute of the building process, but looking back, those were some of the best times of my life. We'd gone way off-grid, but we were onto something with our little world out there in the woods. We were together, family was the focus, and distractions were few. We had created a refuge of love and adventure in that little cabin in the woods. I realize now that I owe a lot to that place. Scott was right: there was something better out there.

CRAWFISH MAC ᴀɴᴅ CHEESE
❧ *Serves 8* ❧

4 cups macaroni

4 tablespoons (½ stick)
    unsalted butter

2 onions, chopped

6 garlic cloves, finely chopped

1 teaspoon cayenne pepper

1 anchovy fillet

1 cup dry white wine

¼ cup all-purpose flour

4½ cups milk, warmed

2 teaspoons prepared
    yellow mustard

1 cup grated aged
    cheddar cheese

1 cup grated Parmigiano-
    Reggiano cheese, plus extra
    shavings for garnish

1 cup grated Gruyère cheese

1½ pounds crawfish tail meat,
    cooked, peeled, deveined,
    and chopped

2 green onions, sliced,
    for garnish

2 red jalapeño peppers, sliced,
    for garnish

Crusty bread, for serving

Tossed green salad, for serving

Preheat the oven to 350°F.

Bring a large stockpot of water to a boil over heat and cook the pasta according to the package instructions until al dente. Scoop out some of the pasta water with a mug or measuring cup, then drain the pasta.

In a Dutch oven, melt the butter over medium heat. Add the onions and sauté for about 4 minutes, until soft. Add the garlic, cayenne, and anchovy fillet and cook for another 5 minutes, breaking the anchovy apart with the back of a wooden spoon. Add the wine and allow to reduce by half.

Reduce the heat to low, stir the flour into the onion mixture, and cook for about 2 minutes. Add the warm milk and mustard and stir until smooth. Allow the sauce to thicken for 2 to 5 minutes, but keep it a little loose—when it begins to barely coat a spoon, take it off the heat.

In a medium bowl, mix the cheeses together. Add 2 cups of the mixed cheese to the sauce and mix well. Add the macaroni and chopped crawfish meat. Mix well and correct any seasonings. If the mixture is too thick, add a little of the reserved pasta water. The sauce needs to be loose as it will thicken in the oven.

Scatter the remaining 1 cup cheese over the top. Bake until golden and bubbly, 35 to 40 minutes. Remove from the oven and allow to sit for about 10 minutes before serving. Garnish with green onions, jalapeño slices, and Parmigiano-Reggiano cheese. Serve with crusty bread and a salad.

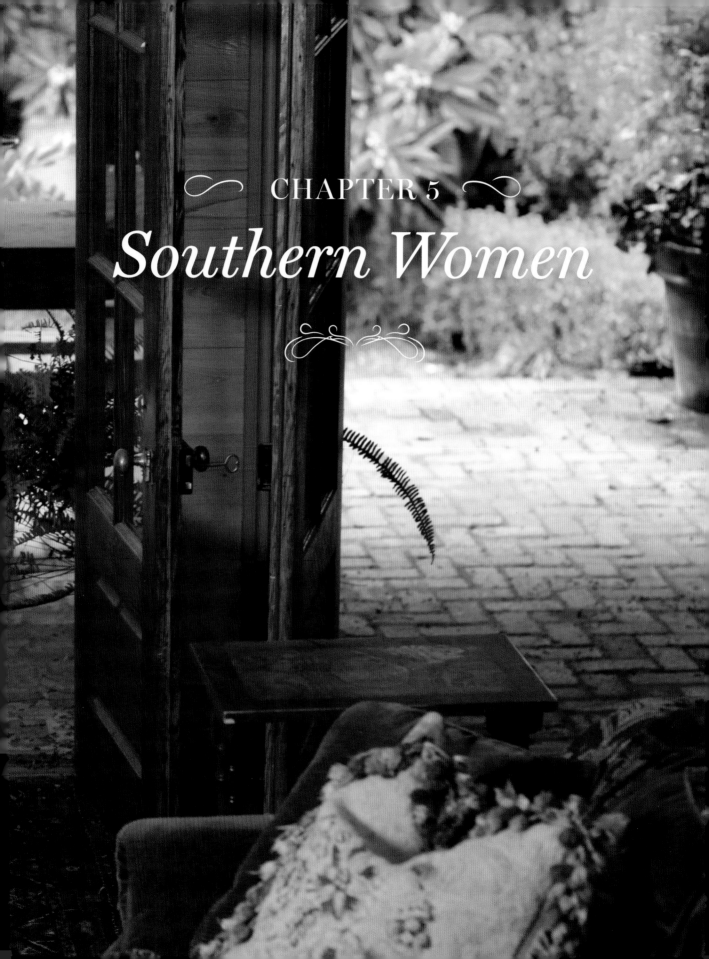

CHAPTER 5

Southern Women

Southern women are as sweet as sugar, as gentle as doves, and as charming as a cottage planted in the middle of a flowered meadow . . . until they're not. With a cut of their eyes, they can pierce right through your soul and rip your heart out. Fierce, strong, hot-headed, and clever are also adjectives that describe us well. I learned how to manage these dual sides by watching one of the best in action: my mother.

Like most Southern girls, I was first and foremost taught manners, etiquette, obedience, and the Golden Rule, aka, to treat others as I would want to be treated. Etiquette classes, taught at Gayfers, a local department store, were a must for every young girl. I have to say,

hardworking women. Neither of their lives have been easy, and both have been forced to be strong, for which I am grateful. Meme was the vice president of an insurance company in the late 1950s and '60s, which was an extremely rare position for a woman, and my mom was Alabama's Postal Service district manager, also a rare position for a woman. Both were always neat, with short hair and minimal but stylish makeup, and very ladylike. Every morning, Mom walked out of the door with a pressed skirt and jacket or pantsuit, low heels, and pocketbook on her arm. She was lovely, elegant, and suited for business. My theory is that by being the hardworking ladies they were teaching me to be, they were able to gain

A Southern woman is as sweet as tea . . . until she's not!

even though I was a tomboy of sorts, I adored the etiquette classes; those classes taught me that manners aren't merely silly rules for acceptance. They are about making others feel welcome, comfortable, and loved, and I'm thankful we learned those lessons.

My mom wasn't going to leave my training all to others, though. As I got older, she relentlessly taught me how to incorporate boldness, strength, and cleverness into the manners and gentleness I'd learned. We're friends now, but growing up, I will say, she was Mom first, and rightfully so. Often, she'd say to me, "I'm not here to be your friend. I am your Mom and always will be. I will tell you the truth and put you straight. That's my job."

My mom, and her mother, Meme, were extremely strong, capable, energetic,

the respect of those who hired them for these outstanding positions. If I can teach my girls even half of what my mom taught me, they'll be ahead of the game.

Hard work was required. Your best work was required. Laziness was not tolerated. Boredom was not permitted, nor was wasting time. To this day, I still have a hard time taking a nap, or not being occupied in some useful way. The only time I take naps is right after a baby is born, and I consider napping as work: it's to stay in a good mood while raising the rest of the kids and dealing with a newborn. Though it seems that my mom's expectations for me may have been unusually high, her only real expectation was that I try my hardest at every endeavor and that I stand up for others, as well as myself.

I can hear her now: "I think I taught you too well how to be kind, Stacy. There's a time to stand up for yourself and for those who can't stand up for themselves. It must start with you." She knows that a woman must find that fine balance between her gentleness and kindness and her clever intelligence and courageous boldness. Mom taught me that being a true Southern lady includes making my voice heard and opinions known on matters of unjustness, and as much as will allow, expressing that injustice along with its solution with kindness, strength, resolve, and passion.

She made it clear to me that I must care more about what's on the inside than the outside. "Appearance is fleeting, but character remains" is her mantra. Character is what matters, not only in myself but others.

Mom's skill for maneuvering seamlessly through her priorities was epic. Though she worked full-time and traveled all over the country for her job, she made it to all of my events—and boy, did I have a lot of them. I never doubted she would make it to cheerleading tryouts, an important speech, or recitals, even if she happened to be halfway across the country. She made arrangements, no matter the cost, to be there.

I remember one recital quite well. When I was six years old, right before a dance recital, an instructor informed my mom that I would not be performing because I hadn't attended a rehearsal that the instructor had misdated. We, along with another dozen or so performers, had shown up the night before as per instructions, but the doors were locked, and the instructor wasn't there. The parents thought there might have been an emergency and the instructor couldn't make it. We all showed up for the recital excited and ready to perform. Upon the instructor's news that I wouldn't be performing, the tiger in my mom was beginning to emerge. There was no way we were walking out of there without me performing in a recital for which I'd worked all year. The entire recital stopped, and you could hear a pin drop as my mom and the instructor "worked things out." As I got on stage, it seemed like the entire crowd went wild. They loved my mom getting justice. I will say if it truly had been unjust that I perform, she would have been the first to admit it and acquiesce. There's nothing that brings out Southern hotheaded fierceness like the loyalty of a mother, or injustice executed on the innocent.

After the stress of that day, how she managed to get a perfectly cooked roast and potatoes on the table, I'll never know. She never claimed to be the best cook, or even a good cook, but by gosh, we had dinner on the table every night. This is another example of the relentless loyalty and care placed on her number one priority: her family.

It is true, there are two sides to the Southern lady. Though she'd rather be traditionally feminine, amiable, charming, and considerate, her loyalty, honor, pride, and desire for rightness will bring out the fierce strength of a tigress as fast as you can say, "Katy bar the door!" That's what the Southern lady is all about!

ULTIMATE POT ROAST AND CREAMY GREAT NORTHERN BEANS

◦~ *Serves 8–10* ~◦

5 tablespoons olive oil, divided

1 (3-pound) chuck roast or venison hindquarter (see Stacy Lyn's Notes, page 104)

1 tablespoon kosher salt, plus more for seasoning

2 teaspoons freshly ground black pepper, plus more for seasoning

All-purpose flour, for dredging

5 medium carrots, chopped

5 celery stalks, chopped

2 Vidalia or yellow onions, chopped

4 garlic cloves, minced, divided

½ cup dry red wine, such as Burgundy or cabernet sauvignon

1½–2½ cups beef stock

2 tablespoons Worcestershire sauce

6 thyme sprigs

1 teaspoon red pepper flakes

2 (15-ounce) cans great northern white beans, rinsed and drained

3 tablespoons chopped fresh parsley, for garnish

1 sliced red chile pepper, for garnish

Squash Relish (page 78), for serving

(continued)

Preheat the oven to 325°F.

Heat 2 tablespoons of the oil in a Dutch oven or casserole dish over medium-high heat until shimmering. Pat the roast dry with a paper towel and season liberally with salt and pepper. Put the flour in a large bowl and dredge the roast in the flour. Brown the roast in the hot oil, 4 to 5 minutes on each side. Transfer the roast to a large plate.

Add the remaining 3 tablespoons oil to the Dutch oven and turn the heat down to medium. Add the carrots, celery, and onions and sauté for about 5 minutes. Add three-fourths of the garlic and cook for about 1 minute. Add the salt and pepper. Add the wine, 1½ cups stock, and Worcestershire sauce to deglaze the pan.

> **Stacy Lyn's Notes**
> It's a comfort food that can feed a crowd! If you are using venison, add an extra hour to the cook time. For each additional pound of beef or venison, also add an hour to the cook time. I think you're going to find this dish one of your "keepers."

Return the roast to the Dutch oven. Place a few thyme sprigs on top of the roast and the remainder of the sprigs in the liquid. Cover and bake for 2 hours. After 2 hours, check the roast. If most of the liquid has been absorbed, add the remaining 1 cup stock. Turn the heat down to 250°F, cover, and bake for another hour, or until the meat is fork-tender.

When the roast is nearly done, make the beans. In a medium saucepan, add a tablespoon of olive oil and cook the remaining garlic and the red pepper flakes over medium-high heat for about 30 seconds. Add the beans and bring to a boil, then reduce the heat and simmer for about 15 minutes. Season with salt and pepper.

Remove the roast from the oven and allow it to rest for about 10 minutes, then slice the meat or shred it with two forks.

To serve, ladle some beans into individual shallow bowls. Spoon some of the roast and vegetables over the beans. Garnish with the parsley and red chiles and serve with the squash relish.

CRUNCHY, CREAMY PARMESAN ROASTED POTATO WEDGES

❧ *Serves 10* ❧

3 tablespoons olive oil

3 tablespoons cornstarch

¾ cup hot water

7 medium Yukon Gold potatoes, each cut lengthwise into 8 wedges

¼ cup kosher salt

½ cup grated Parmigiano-Reggiano cheese

3 tablespoons chopped fresh parsley, for garnish

Preheat the oven to 425°F. Line a rimmed baking sheet with aluminum foil and coat with the olive oil.

In a small bowl, whisk together the cornstarch and hot water. Place in the microwave and cook for 90 seconds, or until a paste has formed. Rub the cornstarch paste all over the potato wedges.

Spread out the potato wedges on the prepared baking sheet. Be sure not to crowd the potatoes or they will steam and not brown. Cover with foil and roast for 10 minutes. Remove the foil and roast for another 15 minutes. Flip the potatoes and roast for another 15 minutes, or until the wedges are golden brown and tender.

While still piping hot, sprinkle the potatoes with the salt and Parmigiano-Reggiano cheese. Garnish with parsley. Serve right away.

CHAPTER 6

Celebrations Are Worth Celebrating

Southerners love to celebrate. Anything. And everything. We celebrate anything from a promotion at work to our dog's birthday. Big events commemorating a new life achievement, such as weddings, graduations, or a new baby, are some of our favorites for gathering and sharing the best food known to man. There is nothing more important to the Southerner than family life, community, and, of course, food, making Southerners and celebrations the perfect fit.

Sure, celebrations take time to plan, but I've never regretted planning or participating in any of them. It's a way to honor one another and express love and value toward those who

Celebrations and Southerners are like sugar and iced tea; the two are just made for each other.

are important to us. Celebrations, whether big or small, allow a set time to break from the humdrum of life and relate with family and friends—"to be all there," as I like to say.

Celebrations like football game days aren't formal events but are gatherings that can be counted on every year. They give life a framework we can depend on and pen into our calendars. For instance, every year, there *will be* a football game between Alabama and Auburn. It's a fact. The only questions are "Who will be hosting the game, and what will we be eating?" or "What food should we take to the tailgate party?" The community gets hyped up, friends discuss plans, and one thing's for sure: there will be food.

There are particular foods that must make it to the party, depending on what celebration you're attending. Weddings, graduations, and showers will be accompanied by perfectly delectable Southern finger foods, while game day celebrations require slightly heavier foods, such as chicken wings, burgers, and fried pickles. Birthdays are always accompanied by a cake or a less traditional pastry, like pie.

Celebrations and Southerners are like sugar and iced tea; the two are just made for each other. Looking forward to game days and birthday bashes bestows excitement, belonging, and a sense of community that Southerners live for. Now, let's go celebrate!

Game Day: It's No Joke

Streets are empty. Downtowns are like ghost towns. You can get a seat at any restaurant in town—unless it's got TVs that are playing the game. Southerners take college football seriously. I often wondered if I were to go into labor during a college football game if my doctor would tell the nurses to do what it takes to stop progress of delivery until the game is over. I'm not kidding here.

I grew up in Alabama, where Alabama–Auburn football games are about as big as Christmas. Talk and preparations begin well pickles, fried okra, fried wings, and whatever else you can find to fry. Families share food, kids throw footballs, truck stereos blare tunes so loud you'd think the lead singer is sitting in your lap, and friends gather, exchange stories, and play games. This is what Southerners wait for all year—fall is football and football is life.

Because dove season and football season intersect, and we are married to the hunt, our family will host a dove shoot during at least a few of the college games. It's perfect that dove hunting doesn't require silence. Radios

> College football is a Southern passion that our kids see and love, making game days a tradition that will eventually become our children's tradition with their own families. I say whatever brings our families and communities together over great food, that's a good thing.

before the day of the big game. If you aren't going to be at the game or tailgating outside the stadium with the other millions of people, you will be at someone's home or hosting game day in your own home with fans from both teams centered around the biggest screen you can find.

If you are tailgating, you'd better live by the mantra "the early bird gets the worm." So early, in fact, that experienced tailgaters start the night before the big day with grills and fryers set up right outside the trucks. There will be several coolers full of drinks, food for preparing burgers, BBQ ribs, pies, dips, chips, fried and iPhones blare every play of the game, and the hunt can go on. Boiled peanuts, cookies, drinks, charged iPhones, guns, binoculars, and a tree to lean up against while watching the sky for doves is a little piece of heaven to the sportsmen in the field.

If I'm not hunting, I'm usually frying wings for after the hunt, or delivering extra drinks to the hunters in our souped-up mini truck outfitted for hunting—in other words, painted camo. Passionate yells from the field that sometimes scare the life out of me let me know every time a score is made, so there's no need for me to listen to the game. I'm just always hoping a fight doesn't break out in the middle of the dove field arising from those passionately supporting opposing teams!

Last year the Alabama–Auburn game ended a good bit after dark, so it was still in progress when Scott got home from hunting. As Scott opened the truck door, he heard what he called "savage screams" through the woods from the neighbor's yard. That could only mean one thing: Auburn had scored. Now, don't get me wrong, we still love our neighbors even though they're Auburn fans. Scott got right back in the truck and just sat there. I walked to the truck a little bewildered, hopped up into the cab, and asked, "Why are you still sitting here?" He replied, "I just don't think I can stand to hear all the smack tomorrow at work about Auburn winning"—that's another thing you should know about the game: each team thinks the other's fans are the most obnoxious winners to walk the face of the earth.

The pain is real.

Scott faced his challenge, got out of the truck, and "heard" nothing—perfect silence, music to his ears. At the last minute, Alabama pulled through and made the winning score. Thankfully, work would be bearable, and Scott could get some sleep that night. Yes, this game affects sleep, health, and sanity.

Some may think all the ruckus around college football is crazy, and in all honesty sometimes I do too, but I'm grateful for the passion Southerners have, even about football. It's a passion that our kids see and love, making game days a tradition that will eventually become our children's tradition with their own families. I say whatever brings our families and communities together over great food, that's a good thing. Roll Tide Roll.

PARMESAN FRIED CHICKEN WINGS
with HONEY-GARLIC DRIZZLE
⟡ *Serves 4* ⟡

FOR THE CHICKEN WINGS

Peanut oil or vegetable oil, for frying

1½ cups all-purpose flour

1 cup finely grated Parmigiano-Reggiano cheese

1½ teaspoons ground mustard

1 teaspoon dried oregano

1½ tablespoons kosher salt

1½ tablespoons freshly ground black pepper

1½ cups buttermilk

4 pounds chicken wings (16–20)

FOR THE HONEY-GARLIC DRIZZLE

3 tablespoons honey

2 tablespoons olive oil

Grated zest and juice of 1 lemon

1 teaspoon kosher salt

½ teaspoon freshly ground black pepper

4 garlic cloves, minced

1 cup chopped fresh parsley

To fry the wings, in a Dutch oven or deep skillet, heat about 2 inches of oil over high heat to 350°F. Place a wire rack over a rimmed baking sheet.

In a shallow dish, whisk together the flour, Parmigiano-Reggiano cheese, mustard, oregano, salt, and pepper. Pour the buttermilk into another shallow dish.

Dredge the chicken wings first in the buttermilk and then in the flour mixture, shaking off any excess flour. Place on the wire rack until ready to fry.

Working in batches, fry the chicken in the hot oil for about 10 minutes, turning as needed, until golden brown and cooked all the way through. Meanwhile, wash the wire rack and baking sheet, line the baking sheet with paper towels, and replace the rack. Transfer the fried wings to the rack.

To make the honey-garlic drizzle, in a medium bowl, whisk together the honey, oil, lemon zest and juice, salt, and pepper. Add the garlic and parsley and mix well. Drizzle over the wings and serve hot.

BEST FRIED PICKLES

❧ *Serves 8* ❧

Vegetable oil, for frying

1½ cups all-purpose flour

1½ cups cornstarch

2 teaspoons garlic powder

1 teaspoon kosher salt

1 teaspoon freshly ground black pepper

1 teaspoon cayenne pepper

1 cup buttermilk

2 large eggs

2 teaspoons Tabasco or other hot sauce

1 (16-ounce) jar sliced dill pickles, drained, or 6 to 8 whole dill pickles, cut into ¼-inch slices

Creamy Comeback Sauce (page 153), for serving

In a Dutch oven or deep skillet, heat about 2 inches of oil over high heat to 375°F. Place a wire rack over a rimmed baking sheet.

In a shallow dish, whisk together the flour, cornstarch, garlic powder, salt, black pepper, and cayenne. In another shallow dish, whisk together the buttermilk, eggs, and hot sauce.

Spread out the pickles on a paper towel and pat dry with another paper towel. This helps the batter stick to the pickles.

Dredge the pickle slices first in the flour mixture, shaking any of the excess, and then in the buttermilk mixture. Finally, coat again with the flour mixture.

Carefully place a few pickle slices at a time in the hot oil and fry for about 1½ minutes, until golden. Using a slotted spoon or spider, transfer the pickles to the wire rack. Before frying the next batch of pickles, make sure the oil returns to 375°F. Serve warm with comeback sauce.

CORNMEAL FRIED OKRA

❦ *Serves 6* ❦

Vegetable or peanut oil, for frying

1 cup cornstarch, divided

1 cup buttermilk

1 cup cornmeal

1 cup all-purpose flour

1 teaspoon Cajun seasoning

1 tablespoon kosher salt, plus more for sprinkling

1 teaspoon freshly ground black pepper

¼ teaspoon garlic powder

1 pound small okra, cut into ¼-inch slices

2 tablespoons chopped fresh parsley or sliced green onions, for garnish

In a Dutch oven or deep skillet, heat about 2 inches of oil over high heat to 350°F. Line a rimmed baking sheet with paper towels and place a wire rack over it.

Put ½ cup of the cornstarch in a shallow dish. Pour the buttermilk into a second shallow dish. In a third shallow dish, whisk together the cornmeal, flour, remaining ½ cup cornstarch, Cajun seasoning, salt, pepper, and garlic powder.

Dredge the sliced okra in the plain cornstarch, then transfer to a sieve and shake off any excess cornstarch. Dip the coated okra into the buttermilk, then into the cornmeal mixture, shaking off any excess coating.

Working in batches, add the okra to the hot oil and fry for 5 to 7 minutes, until golden. Use a slotted spoon or spider to transfer the okra to the wire rack. Sprinkle with salt to taste. Garnish with parsley or green onions.

Graduations, Weddings, and Babies

"Oh, heavens to Betsy, the guests are already here. They're early! Are the chafing dishes full of food yet, or do we still have to get that ready? I've got to go get dressed—I'll check everything in just a minute." This is me in the moments before the Happily Ever After Party for my oldest son, Forrest, and his new wife, Becca. Excitement mixed with a bit of panic and apprehension filled us all as the guests began to arrive. The frenzy of the moment was worth the beauty of family and friends enjoying each other and celebrating the marriage of my first son and his wife.

As I joined the festivities, I took a quick moment to reflect on those gathered underneath the sparkling hundred-year-old moss-laden oaks in celebration of the new couple. For that instant, everything seemed right. The laughter, love, and fellowship were almost too much to take in.

It's true that Southerners love to celebrate most everything, but for graduations, weddings, and babies we don't do just one party—we do many. In the South, these milestones are celebrated with teas, showers, and parties

Making monumental and transitional events special is the Southern way.

We'd had a lovely wedding at Becca's home church in North Carolina where her dad pastors and officiated the ceremony, but many of our close family and friends couldn't attend because of travel difficulties, so we threw the newlyweds a reception at our farm out in the boondocks of Alabama. A white tent lined with twinkling lights towered over tables covered with individual pumpkin lasagna, roast beef, and loaded mashed potatoes in martini glasses, along with rustic crackers and toasted baguettes ready to plunge into salsas, white bean dip, and adobo sauce. Olive oil cakes dusted with powdered sugar, homemade Danish pastries, and macerated fruit cups waited patiently on their very own table. And a drink table graced with an heirloom tablecloth championing mile-high flowers was elegantly begging for attention.

that are beautifully arrayed with heirloom tablecloths adorned with candelabras and fresh flowers. Food can be trays of crustless cucumber dill sandwiches, old-fashioned chicken salad sandwiches, dainty pimiento cheese sandwiches, bacon cheddar biscuits with bacon jam, cookies, cakes, brownies, and petit fours, along with Creamsicle punch or strawberry lemonade mixed with Sprite and cooled with a strawberry ice ring. Or the party may be a four-course dinner and a night of dancing. There's a million ways to do a party—and that's part of the fun.

On occasion I've asked myself, "Is all this hoopla necessary, or are we merely sticking to traditions that make us run around like chickens with our heads cut off?" Usually, I say this as I am running around with a tray of finger sandwiches but feeling like a chicken with my head cut off.

And every time, the answer is yes! These events are personal milestones that mark completely new chapters in our lives. With every new chapter there is an enormous transition. And we need events that signify these rites of passage and help people we love enter their new worlds!

This realization was proven to me during the Covid crisis. Forrest, my oldest, graduated from dental school during 2020. After passing the boards, he immediately started work, and there was a bit of a chasm—a dark hole, a letdown; he had worked so hard for so long, and yet there was nothing to mark his graduation as a huge accomplishment and solidify the "rite of passage" as he traveled on to the next step. It gave me fresh appreciation for what these ceremonies and parties can be—propelling each graduate into a new and exciting direction with resolve.

As much as I believe graduation celebrations are necessary, they don't even compare to wedding celebrations. If anything requires a significant mile marker celebration, it's marriage. Two people from different worlds commit to create a world together, forsaking all others, depending only on each other, choosing to walk down the same paths. Your life is no longer your own. In my eyes, marriage is the most important decision, after salvation, to be made on this earth. You choose to make memories, raise a family, experience the same joys, heartaches, excitement, disappointments, and triumphs with each other in this life. Marriage is a beautiful, exceptional, magnificent gift. Bells should ring. Cymbals should clang.

When I say it deserves a "mile-marker celebration," I don't mean it should be marked by who spent the most money or invited the most people. My favorite weddings are in small country churches or in the middle of a Southern landscape. Of course, it should be pretty, but put the focus where it belongs: on the union of two people in love.

Scott and I married in a small white church beside a lake on a cold February morning. The pastor marrying us had been my boss at a church where I was an intern. My mom was my maid of honor, Scott's dad was his best man, and everyone there were very close friends and family. Marriage is intimate; I think the wedding should be too. Our reception was in a lovely lighthouse next to the church. I wish I'd insisted on having shrimp and grits at the reception; that's the only thing that could have made it more perfect.

As soon as the dust settled from our wedding, babies started coming. Though children are the most wonderful gift, life after the arrival of children is forever changed—and that rite of passage must be marked too! I continually marvel at the fact that two people are given the responsibility and ability to create a life for eternity. I'm breathless as I ponder this magnificent privilege and gift from God. Let the games begin! Again, drums should beat, trumpets should blare—a celebration must signify this new beginning and transition into parenthood.

Though the beauty of the South lends itself to striking celebrations, the real beauty is in the heartbeat of its occupants. I cherish the aprons with handwritten sentiments, cards, and a video of advice from special people who took the time to create meaningful, lasting memories thoughtfully and intentionally for me. The thoughtful care and attention to detail demonstrate love in the Southern heart. Making monumental and transitional events special is the Southern way.

PIMIENTO CHEESE
WITH GREEN OLIVES
❧ *Serves 12* ❧

8 ounces cream cheese, softened

2 cups shredded sharp cheddar cheese

½ cup homemade or good-quality store-bought mayonnaise, such as Duke's or Hellmann's

1 cup green olives with pimientos, chopped

½ teaspoon granulated garlic

¼ teaspoon onion powder

⅛ teaspoon cayenne pepper

Kosher salt and freshly ground black pepper to taste

Tabasco or other hot sauce to taste

1 bunch green onions, sliced

In a medium bowl, mix the cream cheese, cheddar cheese, and mayonnaise with a spatula. Add the rest of the ingredients and mix well. Cover and refrigerate until ready to serve.

Stacy Lyn's Note
Don't be tempted to use packaged cheese that is already shredded or it will result in a dry texture. It's more work to buy the block and shred it, but the result is worth it.

OLD-FASHIONED CHICKEN SALAD

✆ *Serves 6–8* ✇

2 carrots, roughly chopped

1 root end of a bunch of celery, plus 1½ cups finely chopped celery

1 yellow onion, roughly chopped

4 garlic cloves, smashed

1 lemon, halved

10 thyme sprigs

Bunch of parsley stems

3 bay leaves

1 tablespoon kosher salt, plus more for seasoning

1 teaspoon freshly ground black pepper, plus more for seasoning

6 bone-in, skin-on chicken breast halves

2 cups homemade or good-quality store-bought mayonnaise, such as Duke's or Hellmann's

¾ cup finely chopped dill pickles

Crackers, bread, or toast, for serving (optional)

Fill a large stockpot halfway with water and bring to a boil over medium-high heat. Add the carrots, celery root end, onion, garlic cloves, lemon halves, thyme, parsley stems, bay leaves, salt, and pepper and return to a boil. Turn the heat down to medium and cook for about 20 minutes, until the vegetables are tender.

Add the chicken and reduce the heat to low. Allow to simmer for 25 minutes, or until the chicken registers 160°F. Remove the pot from the heat and allow the chicken to cool in the broth. Once cooled, transfer the chicken to a cutting board; reserve the cooking liquid to make soup and feed the vegetables to your chickens if you have them. When cool enough to handle, remove the chicken skin and bones and shred the meat using two forks or by breaking the chicken apart with your fingers.

In a large bowl, mix the mayonnaise, chopped celery, and dill pickles. Add the chicken and stir until fully combined. Add salt and pepper to taste. Serve with crackers, on toasted bread, or just plain!

BACON CHEDDAR BISCUITS

❧ *Serves 10–12* ❧

2 cups all-purpose flour, plus more for dusting

1 tablespoon baking powder

¼ teaspoon baking soda

¾ teaspoon kosher salt, plus more for sprinkling

3 tablespoons cold unsalted butter, plus optional melted butter for brushing

3 tablespoons cold vegetable shortening, such as Crisco

¾ cup shredded cheddar cheese

½ cup crumbled cooked bacon (about 8 ounces before cooking)

1 cup buttermilk, plus more for brushing (optional)

Preheat the oven to 450°F. Place a cast iron skillet in the oven while it preheats.

In a large bowl, sift together the flour, baking powder, baking soda, and salt. Work the cold butter and shortening into the flour mixture with a pastry blender until the mixture resembles coarse meal. Add the cheese and bacon and mix until incorporated. Make a well in the center of the flour mixture, then slowly pour in the buttermilk, gently incorporating the buttermilk with your hands until the flour is wet. The dough isn't going to have a form or shape at this point.

Turn the dough out onto a lightly floured surface and fold on top of itself for about 1 minute. Roll or press the dough into a ½-inch-thick rectangle and, using a biscuit cutter, cut out as many rounds as possible. Gather the leftover dough and roll it out to get more biscuits. Carefully remove the skillet from the oven and transfer the biscuits to the hot skillet, making sure the biscuits are touching one another. Put a light thumbprint in the middle of each biscuit to ensure they rise at the same time. Brush the top of each biscuit with buttermilk or melted butter and sprinkle with kosher salt.

Bake for about 10 minutes, until the biscuits have risen and the tops have begun to brown.

Stacy Lyn's Note

You can double—or even triple—this recipe for a quick make-ahead meal! Once you cut the rounds, just place them about an inch apart on a rimmed baking sheet and freeze for 6 hours, or until completely frozen. Transfer the frozen biscuits to a zip-top bag and freeze for up to 6 months. When you are ready to bake the frozen biscuits, remove the amount you need from the bag and place on a rimmed baking sheet or skillet, making sure the biscuits are touching one another. Bake in a 450°F oven for 12 minutes, or until cooked through and golden.

BACON JAM
❦ *Makes 2 pints* ❧

1½ pounds bacon, chopped

1 teaspoon unsalted butter

3 large onions, diced

1 teaspoon kosher salt

¼ cup bourbon

1 cup apple cider vinegar

¾ cup light brown sugar, firmly packed

Pinch cayenne pepper

¼ cup grainy mustard

2 teaspoons balsamic vinegar

2 teaspoons extra-virgin olive oil

In a cast iron skillet, cook the bacon over medium-high heat until golden and crispy, 6 to 8 minutes. Using a slotted spoon, transfer the bacon to a cutting board and let it cool. Leave the fat in the pan.

Add the butter, onions, and salt to the pan. Reduce the heat to low and cook until the onions are translucent and tender, about 10 minutes.

Add the bourbon, cider vinegar, brown sugar, cayenne, and mustard and simmer until thickened, about 20 minutes. Return the bacon to the skillet and stir until incorporated.

Remove the skillet from the heat and add the balsamic vinegar and olive oil. Mix thoroughly and allow to cool. Refrigerate until ready to use. Serve with biscuits, burgers, over greens, or other vegetables and meats.

Whiskey Baby

Do you know that feeling when you want to celebrate something big in your life, but you are afraid no one else will be excited with you? Or worse, they find the news bad? I was once in a situation where I was tempted to keep it to myself, at least for a while. But the person I wanted to share my good news with was my mom, and I can't keep anything from her for very long. Besides, the news was baby number seven and my body would soon tell the story.

Growing up as my mom's only child, I was not expected to have seven children. Really, that children are a gift and heritage from the Lord. It wasn't by accident that we kept having kids; it was very much thought through. Sure, it is hard to have so many little ones running around at your feet and dealing with their little emergencies all day, but we felt an assurance that this was our path. We prayed and trusted that all would fall into place.

With baby number seven beginning to grow inside me, we knew we had to share the good news with Mom. So, we took deep breaths, loaded the kids in the Suburban, and headed

When you pray, trust, and obey, adventures are endless . . . and you never know what you're going to get!

I think my mom was quite shocked when I broke the news of my first pregnancy while in my last year of law school. Each time we became pregnant, Scott and I discussed at length how we were going to break the news to our parents. Scott's parents were a little easier, but my mom was a tougher audience. I'm her only child, and she worries. We had our second son in Birmingham while Scott was in dental school, and we had little to no money. That was a hard one to break to her. The next baby came when Scott and I had just moved back to Montgomery for him to start a dental practice—again, little to no money. Well, you get the drift.

As much as I understand Mom's concerns and trust her advice, Scott and I are convinced out. As I was reading *The Chronicles of Narnia* to the kids, practically screaming so those in the back could hear me, Scott got off a few exits early. We pulled into the parking lot of a local liquor store. "What in the world are we doing here?" I asked. Scott said he'd be right back and left me in perfect bewilderment as he walked through the doors. In just a few minutes, he was headed back to the truck holding a brown paper bag with what looked like a bottle of whiskey inside. I was truly taken aback because we don't drink, and here in the South, churchgoers are known to go out of town to get their Jack Daniel's, wine, and other liquor to cook with instead of risking someone they know seeing them exiting the store with a huge bottle of bourbon.

"Is this for us before we break the news? I can't have it; I'm pregnant. Mom doesn't drink either, so what in the world?" Scott explained that we wouldn't have to say a thing if we just handed Mom the bottle. Nothing else we could say besides "We are having baby number seven" would warrant a strong drink. She'd surely get it. No reasons. No expositions. Just simply hand her the bottle. Genius!

The kids just couldn't wait to see her reaction. And boy does she ever have reactions. We pulled up to her house, piled out of the truck, and headed to the door with the whiskey bottle in the brown paper bag. Greetings were shared, and then the moment of truth. I'll never forget it—all the kids wide-eyed, with huge smiles, some sitting on the living room's dark-green sofa, some standing.

Scott asked Mom to sit down in the red chair next to the sofa in front of the fireplace, then handed her the bag. She opened it and right away knew exactly what it meant! It worked!

The kids busted out laughing, which contagiously spread to Mom and to Scott and me. She loves the kids so very much and handled it like a trooper. I'll bet she still has that unopened bottle somewhere in the house to this day. By the way, most Southerners love to celebrate anything with whiskey!

BOURBON BREAD PUDDING

❧ *Serves 8* ❧

FOR THE BREAD PUDDING

1 cup half-and-half

3 cups whole milk

5 large eggs

2 tablespoons unsalted butter, melted

¾ cup granulated sugar

½ teaspoon ground cinnamon

10 cups torn brioche or French bread (1-inch pieces from a 1-pound loaf)

1 cup chopped pecans, plus more for serving

1 cup raisins (optional)

FOR THE BOURBON SAUCE

1 cup (2 sticks) unsalted butter

1 cup dark brown sugar, firmly packed

3 tablespoons bourbon

½ cup buttermilk

1 tablespoon light corn syrup

1 teaspoon ground cinnamon

½ teaspoon kosher salt

¼ teaspoon grated nutmeg

2 teaspoons vanilla extract

Powdered sugar, for sprinkling

Butter a 13 x 9-inch baking dish.

To make the bread pudding, in a large bowl, whisk together the half-and-half, milk, eggs, melted butter, granulated sugar, and cinnamon until smooth. Pour half of the mixture into the prepared baking dish. Scatter the bread, half of the pecans, and half of the raisins (if using) over the custard mixture.

Slowly and as evenly as possible, pour the rest of the custard mixture over the bread and top with the remaining pecans and raisins. Let the pudding sit for 30 minutes so the bread can fully absorb the milk. Meanwhile, preheat the oven to 350°F.

Bake the bread pudding for 45 minutes, or until lightly browned.

To make the bourbon sauce, combine the butter and brown sugar in a medium saucepan and heat over medium heat, stirring, until the sugar is dissolved. Add the bourbon, buttermilk, corn syrup, cinnamon, salt, and nutmeg and bring to a boil. Boil until heated through, about 1 minute. Remove from the heat and stir in the vanilla. Drizzle the sauce over the bread pudding and top with a sprinkle of powdered sugar.

Stacy Lyn's Note
When blueberries are in season, they are a wonderful substitute for the raisins. Also, toasting the pecans in a 350°F oven for about 5 minutes, until lightly browned, will bring out the pecans' flavor and keep them crunchier.

Birthday Bashes

In the South, birthdays are a big deal. Maybe it's because Southerners just want to celebrate, but I believe it's because we intuitively want to make others feel special. It's not unusual to go to work only to find thirty flamingos on the office lawn in celebration of your thirtieth birthday, or to be invited to your friend's fiftieth surprise birthday party at which you are required to dress up like a princess! Birthdays are meant to be fun, special, individual.

Birthdays are one of my all-time favorite life events to celebrate. Baking birthday cakes, so that we could enjoy the celebrated child. Having a lot of siblings is a wonderful way to grow up, but often individuality can easily get crowded out. Having seven kids, it's easy to see them all as "the kids," but it is important to us that they know we see them as individuals too.

Birthday week is just one of the many fun ideas we've come up with. All week, the birthday boy or girl picks out the food, the cake, and the activities, though sometimes other siblings influence the outcome. Food choices during

Every life is valuable and deserves celebrating. Celebrating birthdays is the perfect time to honor, set apart, and show our love and appreciation for the life of others just because they exist!

enjoying special meals, and making lifetime memories are only a few of the reasons I love to celebrate birthdays. Another reason is that most celebrations center around a holiday, or a special day that involves many other people, but birthdays are focused on one special person. It's the one day we're honored, set apart, and made special just because we exist!

In our family, we celebrate nine birthdays a year, almost every month! Scott and I decided early to intentionally try to create consistent activities that allow us to focus on each of the children individually. For us that meant celebrating with only small gatherings of family and close friends; nothing stressful birthday week are sometimes extravagant, but mixed with simple, but always delicious, fare. Once one of the kids wanted squid-ink pasta! A few repeats and all-time favorites through the years have been venison parmesan, fried catfish and hush puppies, oysters Rockefeller, and always grilled steak with garlic compound butter and double-fried French fries. Dessert choices are endless, but some of the favorites are strawberry cake, cappuccino cake, and tres leches cake, and a host of pies. The cake is always made by the birthday honoree, along with me. As soon as each child could stand and stir, they helped me make their own cakes. This is still our tradition after all these years!

As the kids have gotten older, my heart is warmed as I watch the excitement and anticipation as the siblings pool their money and collaborate on a big gift for their birthday sibling. The thought, creativity, and love that goes into the gifts is enough to make a grown man cry. They know each other so well that they inevitably give the "favorite" gift.

Though we've tried to make birthdays entirely individual, two of our kids, our oldest son and oldest daughter, have the same birthday five years apart. I wasn't sure how well this would be accepted or how we might handle making each of them feel special, but it has never been a problem at all. Forrest and Graylyn have loved celebrating their birthdays together. We give them two weeks. Both are quite creative and have excellent, "expensive" taste, so you can just imagine the feasting that goes on during the month of March for us.

On one occasion Graylyn did get her own impromptu surprise birthday party, and it happens to be one of my favorite celebrations. Graylyn and I were cooking a strawberry cake and listening to music, and I was sharing with her the exciting things I saw happening in her life and in our family. I'd made it a habit of sharing the gospel here and there if it fit the conversation with just a few sentences and then I'd move on, not wanting to put the kids on the spot concerning their faith—just planting seeds. And this time, Graylyn jumped in and said, "I want to make Christ my Savior." You can imagine my joy and surprise! Right then and there, I picked up the phone and called the grandparents to invite them over for a birthday party celebrating her new birth. Who knew that the cake we were making would be for this special occasion! How cool is that?

Whether it be a huge birthday bash or a small intimate dinner with a few friends and family, birthdays should be celebrated. It's one simple way to let our family and friends know how precious they are to all those around them. There's no better way to show love, appreciation, and thankfulness for one another than to celebrate their life!

STEAK FRITES
WITH ROQUEFORT BUTTER
❧ *Serves 6* ❧

6 boneless rib eye steaks
(about 8 ounces each)

2 tablespoons unsalted butter,
melted, plus 4 tablespoons
(½ stick) unsalted butter,
room temperature

Freshly ground black pepper
to taste

2 ounces Roquefort
cheese, crumbled, room
temperature

Coarse sea salt to taste

Double-Fried French Fries
(page 136), for serving

Brush the steaks with the melted butter and season with pepper. Set aside for about
30 minutes, or until the steaks reach room temperature.

In a small bowl, mix the room-temperature butter and Roquefort cheese until
well blended.

Heat a large cast iron skillet over medium-high heat. Liberally salt the steaks. Working
in batches, cook the steaks for about 4 minutes, then flip the steaks and cook for 4
minutes more, or until the temperature reaches 135°F.

Transfer the steaks to a cutting board and place a spoonful of Roquefort butter on top
of each. Allow the steaks to rest for about 5 minutes. Serve with fries on the side.

DOUBLE-FRIED FRENCH FRIES:
ALWAYS on the MENU
❦ *Serves 6* ❧

4 large russet potatoes, peeled and cut into ¼-inch-thick fries

3 cups peanut oil, or as needed

Kosher salt to taste

Put the cut potatoes in a large bowl, cover with water, and allow to sit for about 30 minutes.

Heat the oil in a deep fryer or Dutch oven over medium-high heat to 275°F. Line a rimmed baking sheet with paper towels, and another baking sheet with a wire rack.

With a spider or slotted spoon, lower about one-quarter of the potatoes into the hot oil and fry for 5 minutes. Transfer the fries to the paper towels and repeat with the remaining potatoes. Allow the fries to cool completely.

Bring the oil up to 350°F. Add one-quarter of the fries for the second time. Fry for about 5 minutes, until the fries are golden brown. Transfer the fries to the wire rack. Liberally sprinkle with salt. Repeat with the remaining fries.

STRAWBERRY CAKE WITH STRAWBERRY BUTTERCREAM FROSTING

Serves 15–18

FOR THE CAKE

1 pound fresh or thawed frozen strawberries, plus 1 cup mashed strawberries, drained

1 cup (2 sticks) unsalted butter, softened

3 cups granulated sugar

6 large egg yolks

1 tablespoon vanilla extract

4 drops red food coloring

4 cups all-purpose flour, divided, plus more for dusting

4 teaspoons baking powder

1 teaspoon kosher salt

1 cup milk

FOR THE STRAWBERRY BUTTERCREAM FROSTING

1½ cups freeze-dried strawberries

3 cups (6 sticks) unsalted butter

11½ cups powdered sugar

1 tablespoon vanilla extract

¼ teaspoon kosher salt

¾ cup heavy cream

Fresh strawberries, for decoration

Preheat the oven to 350°F. Grease four 8-inch round cake pans with butter, then line the pan bottoms with parchment paper. Grease the parchment with more butter, then dust with flour.

To make the cake, put the whole strawberries in a blender and blend on medium speed until pureed. You will need 1 cup strawberry puree for this recipe; reserve any extra for another use.

In the bowl of a stand mixer fitted with the whisk attachment, beat the butter on medium speed until creamy, about 1 minute. Add the granulated sugar and beat until light and fluffy, about 5 minutes. Add the strawberry puree and mix until combined. Add the egg yolks one at a time, beating until combined after each addition. Add the vanilla and red food coloring and mix until combined.

In a medium bowl, whisk together 1 cup of the flour, the baking powder, and salt. In thirds, add the flour mixture to the butter mixture alternately with the milk, beginning and ending with the flour mixture, beating on low speed until just combined. Fold in the mashed strawberries. Spoon the batter evenly into the prepared pans.

Bake for about 25 minutes, until a toothpick inserted into the center of the cakes comes out clean. Transfer the cakes to a wire rack and allow to completely cool before icing, about 1 hour.

To make the buttercream frosting, in a blender or food processor, process the freeze-dried strawberries until they form a powdered consistency.

In the bowl of a stand mixer fitted with the paddle attachment, beat the butter on medium speed until creamy, about 1 minute. Reduce the speed to low and gradually add the powdered sugar and powdered freeze-dried strawberries, beating for about 2 minutes. Add the vanilla and salt and mix until combined. Increase the speed to medium and slowly add the cream, beating until fluffy.

To assemble the cake, spread a little frosting on the cake stand. Top with one cake layer. Top with about ¾ cup of the frosting, spreading over the top of the layer. Top with a second cake layer and frost the top with another ¾ cup buttercream. Repeat with the remaining layers. Frost the top and sides of the entire cake with the buttercream frosting. Decorate the top with extra whole or sliced strawberries.

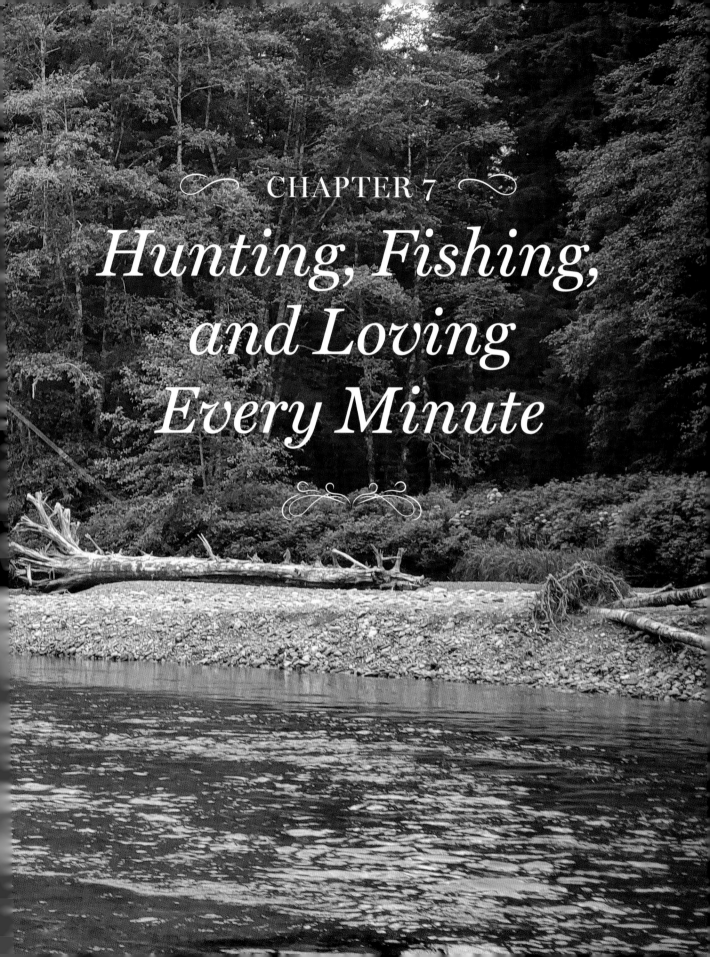

CHAPTER 7

Hunting, Fishing, and Loving Every Minute

Hunting and fishing are an art here in the South. When you see that magnificent piece of art in the gallery that completely captivates you, changes your mood, captures your heart, and makes you feel your life is forever changed—that's what hunting and fishing are to Southerners. Just as a painting evokes passion or a meditative spirit in you, this form of art does as well. No two experiences are ever alike. It never gets old. The beauty never fails.

From the time boys and girls can toddle, they are learning this liberating art. In my case, one of my sons began his fishing baptism the day I brought him home from the hospital. Yes, we commenced Howlett's fishing initiation at

In the South, hunting and fishing are an art— and it's how we "bring home the bacon"!

three days old. Howlett was strapped to me as I baited the hook for the other children and cast a line or two myself.

Because children are initiated into hunting and fishing in the South pretty much from birth, conversation surrounding both hunting and fishing are as common as the weather. Conversations inevitably ensue at the office, church, and even the grocery. The stories never get old, and the art never ends. There are always new techniques, new finds, and new experiences. There's camaraderie and brotherhood between hunters and anglers, much like a fraternity.

If you ask any hunter or angler why they hunt, they might start with the fresh delicious food. But very quickly in the conversation they may declare their love for the way the light plays on the water, or how the light comes through the

trees as the sun rises. They become vulnerable sharing the sounds, sights, feeling, and declaring their love for each beautiful new experience.

It's innate in all of us to work for our food. If there's no meat or fish at the end of their expedition, there was at least that possibility. Even still, the time wasn't wasted. Ever.

As I've experienced my dad, husband, and now sons and daughters hunting and fishing, the simplest way to sum up the results of them fulfilling this ancient art form is this one word: perspective.

Hunting and fishing are the Southerner's way to decompress from the world, gain perspective, bring home the bacon, experience nature, and participate in God's artful creation. It encourages fellowship and camaraderie among all generations. This is what the South is about!

Fishing Holes and Fish Fries

The first memories I have of my dad are of him casting a fishing line in a lake or a nearby neighboring pond. Every chance he could get, he'd be pulling a smallmouth bass or enormous catfish out of the water and putting it in the cooler so it could later be stuffed and roasted or fried to perfection and served with the most crunchy, tender hush puppies known to man.

Dad grew up fishing and winning fishing tournaments. He seemed to instinctively know where the best fishing holes were, what bait to use, and especially how to cook them.

him catching anything in that creek. Maybe, just maybe, his little girl was making too much noise, or better yet, I'd like to think he was enjoying the moment watching me as much as I was enjoying being with him.

Afterwards he'd take me to the tiniest country store slapdab on the corner of a four-way stop, where earlier that morning he'd bought a carton of earthworms to fish with. Dad let me get anything I wanted in the store, and we'd put it on his "tab." I'd get an ice-cold chocolate bottled drink from the chest freezer

I find myself at times trying so hard to make sure everything is just right, the conversations are meaningful and plentiful, and everyone is entertained. But just being there is really all that is necessary. Being there is a love language all on its own.

Around the age of five, I remember him taking me to his favorite creek hidden way back in the woods. The anticipation of walking down the trail and seeing huge rocks just waiting for me to cross over and then to discover a small hidden waterfall was more than this little girl could handle. There was no other place on earth I'd rather be. If you've never swum in a spring-fed creek, just think about jumping into a big glass of ice water and you'll have experienced creek swimming. It's like that all year long—it never warms up!

Dad didn't talk much, but I think he brought me here to be alone with me. He'd cast a line out in the water, but I don't remember

and buttery crackers from the shelves in the back of the store that had smooth, orange cheese on one end of the package and a red stick to smear the cheese all over the crackers. I think I chose that snack over a candy bar because it made me feel like I was "cooking" my own food; it delighted me every time, and I still love that snack today. Maybe that's where my love for all things cheesy made its way into my life. I'd walk right up to the check-out lady and say with bold confidence, "Put it on Wayne's tab please."

After those "fishing trips," Dad would take me to a nearby pond where he *really* caught fish! We'd take the fish home and fry it up

immediately. How could life really get any better than fishing with your dad, then frying up the catch? If we didn't fry it, we'd stuff and grill it. Sometimes we'd blacken it and serve alongside the perfectly ripened vegetables from his weedless garden. He'd even let me make the tartar sauce. I felt like I was born knowing how to make the best tartar sauce, comeback sauce, and any other concoction dad would entrust to me.

Life was simple back then, and I work hard to make sure our family keeps it simple now. It's the best way to live. Just being together is often enough. I doubt Dad knows it, but some of those days were the best times of my life. Just by his being there, making the effort to ensure I was having fun, and of course, letting me "cook" a little with my cheese and crackers snack was enough. I find myself at times trying so hard to make sure everything is just right, the conversations are meaningful and plentiful, and everyone is entertained. But just being there is really all that is necessary. Being there is a love language all on its own.

SOUTHERN CORNMEAL-CRUSTED CATFISH

ᏒᎧ *Serves 6* ᏒᎧ

Peanut or vegetable oil,
    for frying

1 cup all-purpose flour

3 tablespoons seafood
    seasoning, such as
    Zatarain's or Old Bay

1 tablespoon kosher salt

1 teaspoon freshly ground
    black pepper

1 cup buttermilk

2 large eggs

3½ cups yellow cornmeal

6 catfish fillets, rinsed and
    patted dry

Dill Pickle Tartar Sauce
    (page 152), for serving

Preheat the oven to 200°F. Heat 1 inch of oil in a Dutch oven or a deep skillet over medium-high heat to 375°F. Place a wire rack over a rimmed baking sheet.

In a shallow dish, whisk together the flour, seafood seasoning, salt, and pepper. In a second shallow dish, beat together the buttermilk and eggs. Put the cornmeal in a third shallow dish. Dip each catfish fillet first into the flour mixture and then into the buttermilk mixture, making sure to shake off any excess. Press the fish into the cornmeal to coat thoroughly and place on the wire rack. Allow to rest for about 5 minutes before frying.

Working in batches, fry the fish for 3 minutes on one side. Then carefully flip and fry for another 3 to 4 minutes, until golden brown and cooked through. Transfer the cooked catfish to the oven to keep warm. Serve with tartar sauce.

Stacy Lyn's Note
You can store leftover fried catfish in the refrigerator and reheat in a 200°F oven.

BEST CRAB CAKES
⌘ *Serves 12* ⌘

FOR THE CRAB CAKES

2 pounds lump crab meat

1 red or green jalapeño pepper, seeded and minced

6 green onions, finely chopped, plus more for garnish

3 slices bacon, cooked and finely chopped

⅓ cup panko or regular breadcrumbs, plus more for coating the crab cakes

Grated zest of 2 limes (reserve juice for sauce), plus lime wedges for serving

1 tablespoon seafood seasoning, such as Zatarain's or Old Bay

½ teaspoon freshly ground black pepper

1 large egg

5 tablespoons homemade or good-quality store-bought mayonnaise, such as Duke's or Hellmann's

2–3 dashes Tabasco or other hot sauce, plus more for serving

Olive oil, for frying

FOR THE SAUCE

½ cup homemade or good-quality store-bought mayonnaise, such as Duke's or Hellmann's

Juice of 2 limes

2 teaspoons Cajun seasoning

2–3 dashes Tabasco or other hot sauce

Olive oil, if needed

To make the crab cakes, in a large bowl, combine the crab meat, jalapeño, green onions, bacon, breadcrumbs, lime zest, seafood seasoning, and pepper. Gently mix with your hands, being careful to keep some large pieces of crab intact.

In a medium bowl, whisk together the egg, mayonnaise, and hot sauce. Fold the mayonnaise mixture gently into the crab mixture until just combined. Handle the crab mixture as little as possible to keep it from becoming too dense.

Divide the crab cake mixture into 12 equal portions, then form each portion into a patty about 1 inch thick and 2 inches in diameter. Place the crab cakes on a plate and refrigerate for about 1 hour.

Preheat a cast iron skillet over medium-high heat. Add a little oil to the skillet and heat until the oil is shimmering. Working in batches, fry the crab cakes for about 3 minutes, until golden brown on the bottom. Gently turn each crab cake over and cook for 3 more minutes, until golden brown on the other side and heated through. Transfer the crab cakes to a serving platter.

To make the sauce, mix the mayonnaise, lime juice, Cajun seasoning, and hot sauce. If the sauce is too thick, add a little olive oil to loosen it a bit.

Serve the crab cakes with a dollop of sauce, a few lime wedges, a dash or two of hot sauce, and a smile!

NO-FAIL JALAPEÑO CHEDDAR HUSH PUPPIES

Serves 10–12

2 cups self-rising cornmeal

½ cup self-rising flour

2 teaspoons kosher salt, plus more for sprinkling

½ teaspoon freshly ground black pepper

½ cup finely chopped onion

1 jalapeño pepper, finely chopped

½ cup fresh, thawed frozen, or canned corn kernels

1 cup shredded cheddar cheese

1¼ cups buttermilk

1 large egg

4 dashes Tabasco or other hot sauce (optional)

1 quart vegetable or peanut oil

In a large bowl, whisk together the cornmeal, flour, salt, and pepper, removing any lumps. In a separate bowl, mix together the onion, jalapeño, corn, cheese, buttermilk, egg, and hot sauce, if using. Pour the wet ingredients into the dry ingredients and stir well. Allow the batter to stand at room temperature for 10 minutes.

Heat the oil in a deep skillet or deep fryer over high heat to 375°F. Line a rimmed baking sheet with paper towels and place a wire rack over it.

Working in batches, drop the batter by the tablespoon into the hot oil. Once the hush puppies begin to float, 10 to 15 seconds, cook, flipping them occasionally to brown on all sides, until golden brown, about 5 minutes. Transfer the hush puppies to the wire rack and sprinkle with extra salt.

DILL PICKLE TARTAR SAUCE

❧ *Makes 1½ cups* ❧

1 cup homemade or good-quality store-bought mayonnaise, such as Duke's or Hellmann's

2 teaspoons Dijon mustard

Juice of ½ lemon

2 tablespoons dill pickle relish

2 tablespoons finely chopped green onions

1 teaspoon Tabasco or other hot sauce

1 tablespoon drained capers, roughly chopped

Pinch kosher salt

¼ teaspoon freshly ground black pepper

In a bowl, combine all the ingredients. Adjust the seasoning to taste. Cover and refrigerate for about 30 minutes before serving. Store any leftover tartar sauce in the refrigerator for up to a week.

CREAMY COMEBACK SAUCE

Makes 1½ cups

1 cup homemade or good-quality store-bought mayonnaise, such as Duke's or Hellmann's

4 celery stalks, roughly chopped

3 tablespoons grainy mustard

2 tablespoons freshly grated horseradish

2 tablespoons diced onion

2 garlic cloves, roughly chopped

2 tablespoons capers, drained

1 tablespoon chopped dill pickle or relish

Grated zest and juice of ½ lemon

3 tablespoons fresh parsley leaves

1 teaspoon kosher salt

½ teaspoon freshly ground black pepper

¾ teaspoon cayenne pepper

In a blender, combine all the ingredients and pulse until the mixture is as smooth or chunky as you like it. Store in an airtight container in the refrigerator for up to 1 week.

Stacy Lyn's Note
Comeback sauce tastes best a day or two after you make it, so the ingredients have time to blend.

Marriage Is Wild

A big hunk of meat from God only knows where. A whole unscaled fish with eyes staring up at me. A few birds still clothed with their feathers. All on the countertop. What's a girl to do?

I'm a newlywed with my new husband, "Daniel Boone," bringing home wild game meats and fish for me to cook, and I have no idea where to start. Since I didn't grow up with my dad, who hunted and fished, I didn't know anything about cooking with game meats. I did know how to cook fish, but only after it had been scaled and filleted.

engagement for quite some time based on advice, great advice, from his father: "Son, if you can't give up hunting for Stacy, you shouldn't marry her. A man lays down his life for his bride. You will have to do this time and again for her."

Granted, I knew when I married Scott that I had married a hunter. But as a new bride, I didn't know I'd feel in competition with hunting! For the first few years of marriage, things were a little wild during hunting season to say the least. Scott believed by cutting back a

The one thing I knew I could do to delight Scott was to make those applewood bacon–wrapped venison steaks he kept wishing for, along with a surprise wild game breakfast. Being negative about his passion was not an option. When you stop bucking and start bending, you never know what you might find to love!

Actually, Scott was up to cooking what he'd harvested, but I hated the way it tasted and really didn't want him hunting all that much anyway. In Scott's mind, he'd really cut back on his hunting schedule. Instead of going every morning and afternoon, he only went every day on the weekends. He thought this was an exceptional compromise. I didn't. This created quite the problem.

Scott's passion for hunting can't be put into words. I've never met anyone who loves it as much as he does. He even delayed our

bit, that would do the trick. Apparently, not for me. I bucked like a wild stallion whenever he'd announce he was going hunting. Sometimes my bucking was silence, but it was still felt.

One day after praying long and hard in our cozy, small den, I felt that it was time to stop bucking Scott and start bending. I'd always felt that a wife should adapt to her husband, but in this one area, I had been extremely obstinate, and felt he was wrong. I'd felt justified in my stubbornness on this issue because we'd had our first child within thirteen months of

marriage, and I needed a break or at least to have him home with me on weekends.

Ultimately, it didn't matter if he was right or wrong. Bucking my husband had to stop. The one thing I knew I could do to delight Scott was to make those applewood bacon–wrapped venison steaks he kept wishing for, along with a surprise wild game breakfast. Being negative about his passion was not an option. Deciding that his passion could be something we both embraced was the best thing I have ever done in marriage, and I'm now convinced wild game

and fresh fish are the perfect ingredients! When I was a newlywed, I never knew I'd feel this way—but when you are eating venison, life is sweet!

Through my bending with Scott, I've found a love in myself for all things wild—including Scott! Though it scared me to give up the fight, it has become my passion with him. The result: joy, laughter, hard work, fun work, and children who love it, too. When you stop bucking and start bending, you never know what you might find to love!

SHAKSHUKA
ᴄᴀ *Serves 6* ᴀᴄ

2 tablespoons olive oil

1 onion, finely chopped

¼ teaspoon plus a pinch
  kosher salt

4 garlic cloves, thinly sliced

1 pound ground venison or beef

¼ cup finely chopped canned
  chipotle peppers in
  adobo sauce

1 quart tomatoes, diced
  and drained

1 teaspoon ground cumin

1 teaspoon sweet paprika

⅛ teaspoon freshly ground
  black pepper

⅛ teaspoon cayenne pepper

⅛ teaspoon freshly grated
  nutmeg

1 bunch cilantro, roughly
  chopped, plus more
  for serving

4 ounces feta cheese, crumbled

6 large eggs

1 tablespoon honey

2 green onions, thinly sliced

1 jalapeño pepper, thinly sliced

Garlic naan bread, for serving

Greek yogurt, for serving

Tabasco or other hot sauce,
  for serving

In a large deep skillet, heat the oil over medium-high heat. Add the onion and a pinch of salt and cook, stirring often, until soft, about 4 minutes. Add the garlic and cook for another minute. Increase the heat to high and add the ground meat. Cook until browned all the way through, 8 to 10 minutes.

Add the chipotle peppers, tomatoes, cumin, paprika, remaining ¼ teaspoon salt, black pepper, cayenne, nutmeg, cilantro, and feta and stir well. Reduce the heat to medium and cook until slightly thickened.

Make six indentions in the skillet mixture using the back of a spoon. Crack an egg into each indention. Cover and cook for 5 to 7 minutes, until the eggs are cooked to your liking. Drizzle with the honey and sprinkle with the green onions, jalapeño, and additional cilantro. Serve with naan, Greek yogurt, and hot sauce.

> **Stacy Lyn's Note**
> Shakshuka is a Middle Eastern dish of eggs poached in saucy tomatoes, onions, garlic, and spices like cumin, paprika, and cayenne. It translates well as a Southern dish when tomatoes are ripe from the vine, jalapeños dot the entire garden, and herbs are plentiful during the spring and summer months. This has become one of our family's favorite "New South" dishes.

APPLEWOOD BACON–WRAPPED VENISON STEAKS WITH BROWN BUTTER HERB SAUCE

∽ *Serves 6* ∽

FOR THE STEAKS
Kosher salt and freshly ground
    black pepper to taste

1 (2-pound) venison loin, cut
    into 6 (2-inch-thick) steaks

6 slices applewood bacon

2 tablespoons olive oil

2 tablespoons unsalted butter

FOR THE BROWN BUTTER HERB SAUCE
8 tablespoons (1 stick) unsalted
    butter, cut into 1-inch cubes

2 garlic cloves, minced

¼ teaspoon red pepper flakes

2 teaspoons chopped fresh basil

2 teaspoons chopped
    fresh parsley

2 teaspoons fresh thyme leaves

2 teaspoons fresh oregano
    leaves

Grated zest and juice of 1 lemon

Kosher salt and freshly ground
    black pepper to taste

2 ounces shaved Parmigiano-
    Reggiano cheese

To cook the steaks, liberally salt and pepper them all over. Wrap a slice of bacon around each steak and secure with a toothpick.

In a cast iron skillet, heat the olive oil and butter over medium-high heat. Add two steaks and cook for about 3 minutes, then flip the steaks and cook for another 4 minutes, or until the internal temperature reaches 120°F. Transfer to a cutting board and tent with aluminum foil. Repeat with the remaining steaks. Let the steaks rest for at least 10 minutes while you make the sauce.

To make the sauce, wipe out the skillet. Melt the butter in the skillet over medium heat, whisking constantly. Continue to cook and whisk for about 3 minutes, until you see brown bits on the bottom of the pan and the butter turning light brown. Remove the skillet from the heat and stir in the garlic, red pepper flakes, herbs, and lemon zest and juice. Season with salt and pepper.

Ladle sauce over each steak, then top with the shaved Parmigiano-Reggiano.

VENISON AND TURKEY MASALA
✑ *Serves 10* ✑

FOR THE MARINADE AND MEAT

2 teaspoons ground coriander

1 teaspoon ground cumin

1 teaspoon ground turmeric

1 teaspoon ground cardamom

1 teaspoon red pepper flakes

¼ teaspoon ground nutmeg

¼ teaspoon ground cinnamon

⅛ teaspoon ground cloves

1 lemon

6 garlic cloves, minced

1 tablespoon peeled and grated ginger

⅓ cup Greek yogurt

1 (1-pound) venison hindquarter, cut into 1-inch cubes

1 (1-pound) boneless, skinless turkey breast, cut into 1-inch cubes

3 red chiles, sliced

FOR THE MASALA

2 tablespoons vegetable oil

4 tablespoons (½ stick) unsalted butter, divided

2 onions, chopped

4 garlic cloves, minced

2 red chiles, sliced

1 tablespoon ground coriander

2 teaspoons ground turmeric

1 cup chopped fresh cilantro, leaves and tender stems reserved separately

1 (28-ounce) can diced plum tomatoes

⅓ cup ground almonds

2 (14-ounce) cans coconut milk

1 lemon, halved

Kosher salt and freshly ground black pepper to taste

½ cup Greek yogurt

Cooked basmati rice and naan bread, for serving

To marinate the meat, in a small skillet, toast the coriander, cumin, turmeric, cardamom, red pepper flakes, nutmeg, cinnamon, and cloves over medium heat for 1 minute. Transfer the spices to a large bowl. Finely grate in the zest of the lemon and then squeeze in its juice. Add the garlic, ginger, yogurt, venison, turkey, and red chiles. Cover with plastic wrap and marinate in the refrigerator for at least 4 hours, preferably overnight.

To make the masala, heat the oil and 2 tablespoons of the butter in a Dutch oven over medium-high heat until sizzling. Working in batches, add the venison and turkey and cook until browned but not cooked all the way through, about 2 minutes on each side. Transfer the meat to a large bowl.

Melt the remaining 2 tablespoons butter in the same pan. Add the onions and cook over medium-high heat until browned, about 3 minutes. Add the garlic and cook for about 1 minute. Add the red chiles, coriander, turmeric, and cilantro stems and cook for about 3 minutes. Add the tomatoes and give the mixture a stir. Return the turkey and venison to the pan, turn the heat down to low, and simmer for 30 minutes.

Add the ground almonds and simmer for 10 minutes. Stir in the coconut milk and lemon halves and simmer for 15 minutes, stirring occasionally. Remove the lemons with tongs and squeeze the juice into the sauce, then season with salt and pepper to perfection.

Dollop the yogurt on top and swirl it through, then sprinkle with the cilantro leaves. Serve with basmati rice and naan.

Stacy Lyn's Note
This is a splendid dish to cook over an open fire. It's pretty easy to regulate the temperature of the Dutch oven simply by raising it for a cooler temperature and lowering it closer to the fire for a higher temperature. When browning the meat and sautéing the vegetables, place the pot close to the heat; then, once all the ingredients are in the pot, simmer by raising the Dutch oven.

RED PEPPER JELLY–BASTED GRILLED QUAIL
WITH CARAMELIZED PEACHES AND FIGS

Serves 4

½ cup Red Pepper Jelly (recipe follows)

4 tablespoons (½ stick) unsalted butter, melted

4 semi-boneless quail (butterflied)

Kosher salt and freshly ground black pepper to taste

2 ripe peaches, pitted and halved

8 ripe figs, halved

1 tablespoon finely chopped fresh basil

Heat a grill or grill pan over high heat.

In a small saucepan, heat the red pepper jelly over medium heat. Remove 2 tablespoons of the warm pepper jelly to a small bowl and set aside.

Brush the melted butter on both sides of each quail. Liberally salt and pepper the quail on both sides.

When the grill is smoking hot, place the quail breast side up on the grill, brush with the warm red pepper jelly, and grill for 3 minutes. Turn the quail over, brush the cooked side with more red pepper jelly, and grill for 2 to 3 minutes, until golden brown on the other side. Transfer the cooked quail to a plate, breast side up, and spoon the reserved red pepper jelly over each.

Place the peaches and figs skin side down on the grill for about 5 minutes. Turn the fruit over and cook the peaches for 3 to 4 minutes and the figs for 2 minutes or until the fruit is easily pierced with a sharp knife. Transfer the fruit to a plate and top with the chopped basil. Divide the quail, peaches, and figs among four plates. Serve with whole-grain rice and grilled corn slathered with butter.

RED PEPPER JELLY
⌒ *Makes six 8-ounce jars* ⌒

1 pound red jalapeño peppers, stems removed, halved lengthwise, and seeded

1½ cups apple cider vinegar

6 cups sugar

1 tablespoon unsalted butter

1 (3-ounce) packet liquid pectin

Pinch kosher salt

Prepare six pint-size canning jars for canning.

In a food processor, pulse the peppers seven or eight times, until roughly chopped. Transfer the peppers to a large pot and add the vinegar. Bring the mixture to a boil, then lower the heat and simmer for 20 minutes.

Add the sugar and salt to the pepper mixture and bring to a rolling boil, then allow it to continue boiling for 1 minute. Add the butter to keep the mixture from foaming. Add the liquid pectin and stir. Allow the mixture to boil for 3 minutes, then remove from the heat.

Ladle the mixture into the prepared jars, leaving ¼ inch headspace. Wipe the rims clean, place the hot lids on the jars, and firmly screw on the bands. Process using the hot water bath canning method for 10 minutes. Place the jars on a kitchen towel and allow to come to room temperature.

CHAPTER 8
Car Washes, Cook-Offs, and Potlucks

Southerners love being with each other and will look for every opportunity to do so, especially if it means helping a neighbor. The sentiment Clairee (Olympia Dukakis) told Ouiser (Shirley MacLaine) in *Steel Magnolias*, "You know I love you more than my luggage," is shared between us all, and we love to show that sentiment as much as we like to say it.

There's not a season of the year that exempts Southerners from gathering and serving one another in some way, whether it be potlucks, cook-offs, car washes, or fundraisers. If one isn't happening, you better bet your bottom dollar one's coming up soon. Churches have potlucks on the schedule because we all know that Mrs.

We Southerners love competition almost as much as we love each other, or maybe it's in our blood. That's probably another reason we love our cook-offs and fundraisers, and even our potlucks! Cook-offs are based on someone winning—that's a given, and the townsfolk love being a part of the process by tasting chilis and casting their votes. Most fundraisers have elements of competition, like vying to be the one who sells the most doughnuts, wrapping paper, or pledges. Potlucks may bring a subtle but very real element of competition too. I know my granny felt like the winner every time her delicious deviled eggs were eaten before anyone else's!

Whatever way you look at it, Southerners put their hearts and souls into loving and helping one another. And we have fun doing it, even with a little friendly competition—it's the Southern way!

Young's homemade fried chicken and Sherry's baked bean casserole and all the other favorites draw us together, unite us, and create solidarity and comradeship. If it's summer, there are car washes on every corner, raising money for schools or church youth trips. In the fall, chili cook-offs dot Southern towns with "chili-heads"—yes, that's a real thing—creating the best chili with tomatoes and beans, and some without chili and beans but instead bookoodles of meat, "the traditional way."

Competition becomes an asset to us Southerners when it pushes us to raise more funds for our favorite charities or helps pay for Mr. Olive's medical bills. It even pushes us to create the best food of our lives for those we love. Whatever way you look at it, Southerners put their hearts and souls into loving and helping one another. And we have fun doing it, even with a little friendly competition—it's the Southern way!

There's a Fundraiser for Everything

"It's your choice. Come right up and pick between this television set or the giant Sugar Daddy Lollipop for second place prize," the announcer said from the auditorium stage. I walked, well excitedly ran—up the side stairs of the stage right toward the prizes, and with no hesitation at all, grabbed my Sugar Daddy Lollipop as fast as a hot knife through butter.

I was in the first grade when I won that unforgettable prize. I'd probably make the same choice today. Who wouldn't rather have a bigger-than-life Sugar Daddy Lollipop than having a cartwheel-a-thon," Coach York said excitedly. I loved the idea. I could do cartwheels for days. This kind of fundraiser is brilliant! I made hundreds of dollars for our gymnastics team by getting about thirty people to make a pledge based on the number of cartwheels I could do in thirty minutes. Some pledged five cents a cartwheel, but some pledged a dollar. I believe some of the pledgers underestimated my love and ability for all things gymnastics! I did over five hundred cartwheels!

Who knew raising money could be so fun?
There may be easier ways to send kids on choir tour
or get that new gym, but the community unites through
fun, inclusive activities that solidify relationships
and create traditions and memories for a lifetime.

a television? It was as tall as I was, and the stretchy, blond candy was as big as my torso and head put together. I'd sell wrapping paper any day for the chance to win that again. And I was doing the selling for a great cause: air conditioning for the school. If you were to spend just one day in Alabama, even during the winter, you would understand the exceptional need for air conditioning.

Soon after the air conditioner fundraiser for my elementary school, my gymnastics coach asked us to get pledges from our friends and family to help pay for the gym. "We're

In the South, there are fundraisers for everything at all times of the year. In summer there are car washes, yard sales, dodgeball tournaments, and shrimp boils to raise money for mission, band, baseball, and cheerleading trips. In the fall there are cook-offs, art shows, and talent show fundraisers for anything from building a new sanctuary to raising money for the needy at Christmas. Whatever the fundraiser is, you can bet it will be profitable and fun.

Some of my favorite fundraisers revolve around food. Bake sales, chili cook-offs, shrimp and crawfish boils, Brunswick stew sales, and brisket sales are only a few of the fundraisers I've been delighted to have a part in. No matter who's raising the money, everyone gets involved. With these kinds of fundraisers, it's not at all difficult to pre-sell cakes, stews, chilis, or whatever is being sold, because it's always going to be great. Heck, people have asked me a year in advance to put them down for three gallons of stew or ten Boston butts.

One scene I absolutely adore is men in long aprons drinking lemonade and chatting about the hickory wood chips they used to smoke the meat as they pull the Boston butts out of the smoker, and several more men wrapping them up as fast as possible for the onslaught of contributors. The laughter, camaraderie, and joy in giving time and energy to make building a new sanctuary possible or providing band uniforms creates a warm, loving atmosphere that brings joy to the saddest of folks. Often there's a bake sale going on at the same time to bring in a little more revenue, and almost everyone who buys a Boston butt also takes home a cake, cookies, or cupcakes.

By far, though, the chili cook-off is the all-around favorite fundraiser of the year. In the South, everyone thinks their family chili recipe is the best. Well, the chili cook-off is the perfect time to put them to the test. Practically the entire town buys tickets to the cook-off to taste all the contestants' chilis, cast their votes, and see who will go down in history for the best chili, which everyone has already self-proclaimed as themselves. "Carl, you don't know anything. Chili ain't supposed to have beans." "You're crazy, Louise, it ain't supposed

to have tomatoes!" are the conversations you'll hear on a regular basis. Booths are set up with small plastic spoons, napkins, and little communion cups for sampling, and people swarm from booth to booth testing and casting their votes. For us, the cook-off starts the fall off with a bang.

Who knew raising money could be so fun? There may be easier ways to send kids on choir tour or get that new gym, but the community unites through fun, inclusive activities that solidify relationships and create traditions and memories for a lifetime. There's nothing like being a part of a team that pulls together to accomplish something for others, then does it again and again year after year. Listening to the contestants yell across the room, "There's always next year—you just wait, I'll be taking that title right out of your hands!" is a reminder of a future full of laughter, fun, belonging, and camaraderie . . . which is, by the way, the Southern way.

BRUNSWICK STEW

❧ *Serves 12* ❧

2 tablespoons olive oil

2 Vidalia or other sweet
onions, diced

3 garlic cloves, minced

4 cups shredded cooked
chicken or rabbit

3 cups shredded pulled pork

2 cups beef stock

1 (24-ounce) can diced
tomatoes

1 (15-ounce) can lima beans,
drained

1 (20-ounce) package frozen
creamed corn

4 ears sweet corn, kernels cut
from the cobs

¼ cup ketchup

3 tablespoons apple
cider vinegar

2 tablespoons light brown
sugar, firmly packed

2 tablespoons Worcestershire
sauce

2½ teaspoons Cajun seasoning

¼ teaspoon cayenne pepper

Juice of 1 lemon

3–4 dashes Tabasco or other
hot sauce

Kosher salt and freshly ground
black pepper to taste

Heat the oil in a Dutch oven over medium heat until shimmering. Add the onions
and sauté for 5 to 7 minutes, until almost translucent. Add the garlic and cook for 30
seconds. Add the shredded chicken and pork, stock, tomatoes with their juices, lima
beans, frozen corn, fresh corn, ketchup, vinegar, brown sugar, Worcestershire, Cajun
seasoning, cayenne pepper, and lemon juice. Turn the heat down to medium-low and
simmer for 45 minutes. Add the hot sauce and season with salt and pepper.

Stacy Lyn's Notes

Always make sure your venison is dry and the skillet is super hot before you brown the meat. Browning enhances the flavor of the dish by giving more depth of flavor. The "secret ingredient" in this award-winning chili is the yellow corn muffin mix; Jiffy Corn Muffin Mix is my favorite. It gives the perfect earthiness to this dish. To make the stew go further, serve over rice.

STACY LYN'S AWARD-WINNING CHILI

ᵜ *Serves 12* ᵜ

1 (16-ounce) can diced
tomatoes

1 tablespoon minced canned
chipotle chiles in adobo
sauce

5 slices bacon, finely chopped

3 pounds venison stew meat
or beef chuck, cut into
½-inch cubes

Kosher salt and freshly ground
black pepper to taste

3 pounds ground beef

2 tablespoons olive oil

1 large onion, chopped

1 jalapeño pepper, seeded and
chopped

1 (15-ounce) can kidney beans,
drained and rinsed

3 tablespoons chili powder

1½ teaspoons ground cumin

1½ teaspoons dried oregano

4 garlic cloves, minced

4 cups beef stock

1 tablespoon light brown sugar,
firmly packed

2 tablespoons yellow corn
muffin mix

Sour cream or shredded cheese
and green onions,
for serving

Fried Jalapeño Cornbread
(page 10), for serving

In a food processor, combine the tomatoes and their juices with the chipotle chiles and
puree until smooth, about 10 seconds; set aside.

In a Dutch oven, cook the bacon over medium heat until crisp. Using a slotted spoon,
transfer the bacon to a paper towel. Leave the fat in the pan.

Pat the venison dry and season with salt and pepper. Heat the fat in the pan over
medium-high heat until smoking hot. Add half of the venison to the pan and brown
on all sides for 6 to 8 minutes. Using a slotted spoon, transfer the venison to a bowl.
Repeat to cook the rest of the venison. Add the beef to the Dutch oven and cook for
10 to 15 minutes, until cooked through. Using a slotted spoon, transfer the beef to the
bowl with the venison.

Add the olive oil, onion, and jalapeño to the pan and cook for about 5 minutes, until
softened. Stir in the kidney beans, chili powder, cumin, oregano, and garlic and cook
for about 30 seconds. Stir in the tomato puree, stock, and brown sugar and bring to
a boil. Reduce the heat to low, add in the bacon, venison, and beef, then cover and
simmer for 1 hour. Uncover, stir, and simmer for about 30 minutes longer.

Ladle 1 cup of the chili liquid into a medium bowl and stir in the muffin mix. Whisk
the mixture back into the chili and simmer until the chili thickens, about 15 minutes.
Check the seasonings. Top servings with a dollop of sour cream or shredded cheese and
serve with cornbread, extra jalapeños, chopped onions, and green onions.

Potluck Lunches

Potluck lunches are a regular occurrence in the South, especially in the Southern church. Each family brings their favorite dish to share with the other families. Everyone enjoys each other's company while devouring the diverse dishes without reservation. The camaraderie within the congregation seems to grow more over food than any other way, making the potluck lunch on the top of the list for events promoting fellowship that should be consistently held. Beware: sometimes that consistency can lead to a little weight gain.

next potluck and give me plenty of advance notice so I could be there too. Besides meeting the preacher, I believe her greatest desire was for me to see how her food compared with the others, knowing hers was the best. I did love seeing her beam with pride! "Look, Stacy, all the deviled eggs are gone. And the ambrosia too. I just can't make enough of anything," Granny would slyly say, smiling as proud as a peacock.

There's always a bit of friendly competition involved in the potluck, and it's quite reasonable

> I've learned more about the people, made incredible lifelong friendships, and even started a new career by going to potluck lunches! I'm convinced the perfect way to get to know new people is over a plate full of food.

"I've gained thirty-five pounds this year from potluck lunches," Preacher Joe, my daughter-in-law's grandfather, nonchalantly said to Becca. He continued, "I had to try every single dish. All the ladies and a few of the men brought their favorite family recipes that I just 'had' to try, and now it's showing up right here," as he rubbed his belly. I've never viewed potlucks from the preacher's perspective before, but it sure makes a lot of sense.

My grandmother practically worshiped her preacher, and insisted on him trying her deviled eggs, fried chicken, and ambrosia—all on the same day. My grandmother would plan for weeks what she was going to take to the

since favorite family recipes are somewhat expected. You can see the cooks eyeing the preacher's plate and then cutting their eyes toward the table to see if people are going for seconds of the dish they'd prepared. Lots of chatter ensues about getting Mrs. Jones's squash casserole recipe or just how moist Liz's five-flavor pound cake is. Toward the end of the potluck, the merciful members make their way back to the table to check that everyone's dish has at least been tried, so no feelings get hurt.

There are also a few rules that must be followed. They aren't verbalized, but eyebrows will be raised if you don't mind your manners. First, bring enough food to feed your own

family. This ensures that there will be enough food to go around. Second, bring homemade, or at least make it look like it's homemade! If you don't have time, it's tolerable to buy something, but what the congregation really wants is a famous recipe handed down through the family. Third, try to eat a little bit of everything and brag about what you love.

One of my favorite potlucks occurred at a church we were visiting in southern Tennessee. After the church service, we were invited to attend a potluck lunch, which we gladly agreed to. We talked all afternoon about everything from raising kids, work, and gardening to publishing. How we got on the topic of publishing, I can't remember, but our new friends encouraged me to stop stalling and get on with writing the book I'd been telling them that I wanted to write. As soon as I buckled the kids into their seatbelts and Scott got on the interstate back to Alabama, I pulled out my notebook and pen and created the outline for my first book. I had finished the introduction by the time we pulled into the driveway. The rest is history!

There's no getting around it: eating with people is intimate. Potlucks are a way to feed that intimacy and create community over a plate of food that everyone helped create. No doubt you will leave full and satisfied from a potluck dinner, but you also may just leave with lifelong friends—and, who knows, a new career!

DISAPPEARING DEVILED EGGS

❧ *Serves 16* ❧

8 large eggs

¼ cup homemade or good-quality store-bought mayonnaise, such as Duke's or Hellmann's

2 tablespoons very finely chopped celery heart (about ½ stalk)

2 tablespoons dill pickle relish

½ teaspoon prepared yellow mustard

⅛ teaspoon kosher salt

Freshly ground black pepper to taste

Toppings: chopped avocado and tomatoes, sliced ham and minced chives, crumbled bacon and sliced jalapeños, or paprika (optional)

Put the eggs in a single layer in a large saucepan and cover with about 3 inches of water. Bring to a boil, then turn off the heat, cover the pan, and set aside for about 15 minutes. Use a slotted spoon to transfer the eggs to a large bowl filled with cold water and ice.

When the eggs are completely cooled, tap each egg on all sides until the entire eggshell is cracked, then peel under cold running water.

Slice the eggs in half lengthwise and remove the egg yolks. Put the egg yolks in a medium bowl and mash with a fork. Stir in the mayonnaise, celery, relish, mustard, salt, and a grind or two of pepper and mix well. Spoon the yolk mixture into the egg whites or use a pastry bag to pipe the filling into the whites. Sprinkle with toppings as desired.

Stacy Lyn's Note
I love to have a little fun decorating the deviled eggs! Adding unexpected elements with toppings of bacon and jalapeños, ham and chives, avocado and tomatoes, or simply a few sprinkles of paprika elevates this side dish to a whole new level!

AMBROSIA

⋅ *Serves 12* ⋅

½ cup maraschino cherries

1 cup heavy cream

2 tablespoons powdered sugar

½ cup sour cream

1 (10-ounce) bag mini
   marshmallows (about 5 cups)

2 cups unsweetened shredded
   coconut

1 pineapple, peeled, cored, and
   cut into cubes

1 cup canned mandarin orange
   segments, drained

1½ cups chopped toasted
   pecans

1 cup seedless green grapes,
   cut in half

Put the maraschino cherries in a strainer and rinse with cold water. Allow to drain for
about 30 minutes.

In the bowl of a stand mixer fitted with the whisk attachment, whip the cream and
sugar until stiff peaks form. Add the sour cream and whisk to combine.

Add the cherries, marshmallows, coconut, pineapple, orange sections, pecans, and
grapes and gently mix with a spatula. Transfer to a serving bowl, cover, and refrigerate
for 30 minutes before serving.

> *Stacy Lyn's Note*
> Nothing's worse than a watery ambrosia! To keep it all sharp and fresh, drain all the fruit before
> adding it. If you are making this ahead, wait until you are ready to serve the dish to add the
> mandarin oranges and toasted pecans.

CHAPTER 9

A Good Man Is Hard to Find

Finding love in the South isn't quite as easy as one might think. It may shock you, but all Southern men are not the same. There are more kinds of Southern men than there are flavors of ice cream. Certainly, there are the farmers as depicted in the movies, but there are businessmen, builders, architects. There are bearded long-hair country boys and the clean-cut city slicker. What's a Southern girl to do?

Well, there is one thing all these men have in common. I've never known a Southern man who didn't like to eat! Thankfully, I found my solace in the kitchen making pastries in my younger years, and then graduating to flounder, BBQ chicken, and bananas Foster. So, I figured out how to snag the guy; now I just needed to find him.

my college Bible Study teacher and now my father-in-law.

All these men contributed in some way to helping me find the ideal man to love. There were a few things I could count on in all these men: they'd drop everything if I needed them, they were all hard workers, they lived by the Southern laws of respect, and of course, they loved good food.

My dad could do anything: garden, hunt, fish. He drove a pickup truck and steered the wheel with his right hand as his left elbow was propped half out the window. This may seem irrelevant, but I don't think so. Scott does that very thing. There's nothing Dad can't fix or build. He's quiet, but when he says something, you'd better listen—it's going to be important.

It may be hard to find a good man, but when you do, you'll know it!

They say a girl marries someone like her dad and chooses a man who loves her like he does. I'm not sure this is 100 percent correct, but for me there's some proof in the pudding. There have been a few extraordinary men in my life who influenced my thoughts on the definition of a good man.

My dad, a celebrated Vietnam vet and power company lineman. My stepdad, a Green Beret and truck driver when Smokey and the Bandit were the coolest things since ice cubes. My grandfather, ex-Navy and a homebuilder. Mr. Brewbaker, owner of the car dealership where I had my first job and my high school Bible Study teacher. And Andy,

My stepdad was strict and had endless advice. I can still hear him lecture: "Don't give a boy the time of day if he doesn't walk closest to the street where traffic is passing, doesn't open doors for you, isn't courteous to waiters and waitresses, doesn't shake hands 'like a man' (I even do that!), or isn't on time. He must be courteous and hardworking, look people in the eyes, and protect you at all costs." I am ever thankful for these lessons.

My grandad, like my dad, was quiet. He rarely said a word, but you knew where you stood by the look on his face. He worked hard, and it showed on his wrinkled but quite handsome face. He never failed to tell me, "Stay

out of the sun, or you'll look like this!" This was his way of telling me he loved me.

Mr. Brewbaker loved lots of things, mainly God and great food, and he stepped in as my dad on a few occasions. He was one of the most "authentic" men I'd ever met. I knew I wanted the man I married to be "real" like him. Anything you'd ask, he'd answer in complete honesty. His voice was gruff from smoking, but that didn't make his words any less impactful. His love for all kinds of foods certainly made an impact on what I do today and on the man I chose. He'd take me and a few of the other employees out to eat lunch at some unique places, encouraging us to "try the lobster" or "order the rib eye."

Once I started dating, I made a checklist with all the advice I'd received from these men about finding a good man, along with characteristics I found in all these men. I used that checklist to a tee. If a guy didn't hold the door open for me, or was disrespectful to a

teacher, or as my dad would say, "that dog don't hunt," meaning he wouldn't work, that was the end of that. My grandmother felt the same way. She told me she would just sit in the car until her date would open her door for her. She once had a guy walk all the way up to the restaurant and had to turn right back around to get his date. I've never forgotten that story!

Soon after I met Andy, my future father-in-law, I met Scott. Interestingly, I met Andy when he came to teach Bible Study for the Fellowship of Christian Athletes at my high school. I can say that man loves God more than life. What's more, he loves his wife more than life too. I wanted a man much like that. Soon I would discover that Scott, his son, was that man. He had all the Southern characteristics I'd compiled on my list. He loved God, worked hard, fixed things, loved the outdoors, could hunt and fish, was highly intelligent, witty, good looking . . . oh, and he loved *all kinds* of food—and me!

Yogurt, BBQ, DQ, Repeat

I thought I'd never again find love, or even happiness, after being heartbroken over the ending of a relationship I thought would last forever. Thankfully, I was wrong. Life did go on, and there was one handsome boy in it!

Sitting on the floor, middle front, in the apartment complex clubhouse with a few friends waiting for Bible Study to start, I eye one of the cutest boys I'd ever seen. Seriously. I'm pretty sure he notices me but am quite sure of it after Bible Study ends. As he heads straight toward me, butterflies fill my stomach

I did know this—my favorite times were *always* those I spent with him. Some of our favorite dates included BBQ and eating contests. Southern girls aren't afraid to eat and can hold their own in the amount they eat too. We'd find our favorite booth at Country's Barbecue and ask the waitress, who knew she'd be getting a nice tip upon our departure, to keep the BBQ chicken coming to the table. Though Scott would say it's debatable, I once won the contest by eating four whole chickens! My strategy was to pass on the "sides," while Scott would fill up

Sometimes life just isn't all that sweet, but if you just wait, it may bring chocolate-covered blueberries!

and a rush of excitement pours over me. "Are you going to TCBY [The Country's Best Yogurt]? We go every week." Ummm, I think to myself, "Are you going to be there? Then yeah!" When he offered a ride in his truck, it was a no-brainer! I hopped up into his black Chevy pickup (as ladylike as possible in a truck with a lift kit) and off we went for chocolate yogurt with sprinkles, my favorite. This was our mode of operation for the rest of the summer.

We spent a lot of time together, and although I was very slow to call it "dating," we sort of were. I knew he met every qualification on my list and more; I just didn't want to rush into a relationship, especially if it was going to brutally end. I mean how can you know?

on them, resulting in my winning the contest!

As full as we were, Dairy Queen would inevitably call our names; my favorite was the Heath Blizzard and Scott's was the Butterfinger Blizzard, but we were up for experimenting with any and all Blizzards. I'd then climb up into that Silverado, him in the driver's seat, windows down and one elbow out of the window, and me in the passenger seat, ponytail through the back of my hat driving the Alabama countryside listening to Hank Williams Jr. on the radio, watching the fields of tall grass blowing in the wind, all while eating ice cream. Great conversation, music, scenery, wind blowing through my hair—how could life get any better? I do believe I was falling head over heels for this man.

I'm not sure of my hesitation, maybe the timing just wasn't right, but I was just noncommittal. So, for the next few years, I'd drive through TCBY religiously, get vanilla yogurt with peanuts (I progressed from the sprinkles), and think about Scott. I'd go out on dates, comparing everyone to Scott without even realizing it. "Scott would never do that. I wonder what Scott would say about this," would keep me up at night. We kept in touch and even had our BBQ eating contests and DQ Blizzards followed by a country drive every once in a while.

Until . . . he came back from Alaska with chocolate-covered blueberries. First, he looked amazing. Second, he brought chocolate-covered blueberries. Third, he noticed something. As soon as he saw the bright red lipstick on my water glass he said, "I've missed that." That's all it took. He had my heart forever.

The rest is history. Marriage, babies, more BBQ, DQ, and drives in the country. I live for these dates, and for the man of my dreams. Pain may be inevitable, but if you let it, life can be sweeter and more "filling" than you can imagine in your wildest dreams.

HOMEMADE PEANUT BUTTER ICE CREAM

⌒ *Serves 8* ⌒

⅔ cup crunchy peanut butter

1 (14-ounce) can sweetened
   condensed milk

1 cup sugar

1 (12-ounce) can evaporated
   milk

2 cups half-and-half

1 cup whole milk

2 teaspoons vanilla extract

Toppings: chopped peanuts,
   chopped chocolate,
   whipped cream, and fresh
   cherries (optional)

In the bowl of a stand mixer fitted with the whisk attachment, mix the peanut butter,
condensed milk, and sugar on medium speed until smooth. Turn the speed down to
low and add the evaporated milk, half-and-half, whole milk, and vanilla and mix well.

Put the bowl in the freezer for 30 to 40 minutes, then pour the mixture into an ice
cream maker and follow the manufacturer's instructions. Eat right away, or for a little
firmer ice cream, put the ice cream in the freezer for 30 minutes. Serve with your
favorite toppings.

BEST-EVER SMOKED CHICKEN
WITH ALABAMA WHITE SAUCE
℃ *Serves 6–8* ℃

FOR THE CHICKEN

¼ cup light brown sugar, firmly packed

1 tablespoon freshly ground black pepper

2 teaspoons kosher salt

2 teaspoons smoked paprika

1 teaspoon garlic powder

1 teaspoon onion powder

1 teaspoon ground mustard

¼ teaspoon cayenne pepper

4 pounds bone-in, skin-on chicken pieces

FOR THE ALABAMA WHITE SAUCE

2 cups homemade or good-quality store-bought mayonnaise, such as Duke's or Hellmann's

½ cup apple cider vinegar

1 tablespoon brown or Creole mustard

1 teaspoon prepared horseradish

1 teaspoon Worcestershire sauce

1 garlic clove, minced

1 teaspoon freshly ground black pepper

½ teaspoon kosher salt

¼ teaspoon cayenne pepper

To smoke the chicken, set a smoker to 225° to 250°F. In a small bowl, combine the brown sugar, black pepper, salt, smoked paprika, garlic powder, onion powder, ground mustard, and cayenne pepper. Massage the spice rub all over the chicken pieces. Put the chicken in the smoker skin side up and smoke until the chicken reaches an internal temperature of 165° to 170°F, 2 to 3 hours. Remove the chicken from the smoker and allow it to rest for at least 15 minutes.

Meanwhile, to make the sauce, in a medium bowl, whisk together all the ingredients until smooth and well combined.

Serve the chicken with the sauce.

> **Stacy Lyn's Note**
> You need to keep these recipes handy. The dry rub can be used on most meats and can be made up to 1 month in advance and stored in an airtight container at room temperature. The Alabama white sauce can be made up to 2 weeks in advance and stored in an airtight container in the refrigerator. Use it on fish, shrimp, and salads, and as a dip for vegetables. At our house, it's always in the fridge!

Southern Honeymooners in Jackson Hole

"Have you got this? I'm going to help your sister down the slope!" aren't the words an inexperienced skier and new husband wants to hear on his honeymoon. The blizzard had gotten us all turned around, and instead of going to a blue slope, Scott and I had found ourselves on a black slope that neither of us were experienced enough to comfortably ski. We were doing all we could not to kill ourselves or anyone else. As if this situation wasn't humiliating enough, the guide, while kindly wanting to rescue me, didn't help by mistaking

Jackson Hole had things he loved too, which gave me an opportunity to learn a little of the give-and-take marriage would require. The National Elk Refuge, which Scott adored, was in Jackson Hole. I'd misunderstood Scott when he prepared me for the sleigh ride that we were going to take through the refuge. The weather was 20 degrees below freezing. He said I needed socks thin enough to allow circulation in my boots. Being me, I thought, well, the thinner the better. That was not at all the correct line of thinking. I wore very thin silk

When you know someone places your interests above their own, you know you're safe.

me for Scott's sibling. This is how our life together began, the two of us on an unexpected adventure with some quirky twists thrown in. We didn't know it then, but we were setting the tone for our whole marriage.

Scott had never been skiing, and I'd been only a few times, but had fallen in love with the sport. I loved everything about it: the snow, the exercise, the strategy, and the fun. Skiing certainly wasn't up Scott's alley, but he wanted me to have everything I wanted. Always listening through the years, he heard clearly that I think the most romantic place in the world is sitting next to a roaring fire when there's snow on the ground. (Very ironic for an Alabama girl, I know.) So, Scott made that happen for us.

socks that had no insulation value whatsoever. I thought I had frostbite for sure! As discreetly as possible on a sled with ten onlookers, I took off my shoes and started massaging the feeling back into my feet. Forget the elk, I'd suddenly become the main attraction. And not in a good way. I guess there was a little embarrassment for us both on this trip.

One solace to my crazy barefoot antics was the food that awaited us after the sleigh ride. We'd had the best latkes that morning, leaving us as full as ticks. I didn't think I'd be hungry again for at least twenty-four hours, but I was wrong. Even though we were miles and miles from Alabama, I felt at home with that evening's dinner of pork scaloppine over greens and grits! And to top it off, bananas Foster for dessert.

Just as the day had begun with theatrics, the night ended with the same—fire reached to the ceiling as the waiter flambéed the dessert tableside. It's a memory that is quite literally burned in my memory!

Through the years, we've often been in unknown territory, and I've always been confident Scott would navigate it as perfectly as any human could. The surprises that have awaited us, good and bad, have been a journey I wouldn't have wanted to miss for the world. Scott has never steered us wrong, and an unbreakable trust has developed through the years that began long ago on our honeymoon. When you know someone places your interests above their own, you know you're in safe, capable hands. Scott optimizes the Southern gentleman: chivalrous, prioritizing loved ones, and demonstrating a can-do spirit. This is the Southern way.

LATKES AND LOX SAUCE
❧ *Serves 4–6* ❧

FOR THE LOX SAUCE

4 ounces cream cheese

½ cup sour cream

3 ounces lox, diced

1 tablespoon sliced
   green onion

FOR THE LATKES

4 russet potatoes, peeled

1 Vidalia or yellow onion

3 large eggs, beaten

½ cup all-purpose flour

2 teaspoons kosher salt

1 teaspoon freshly ground
   black pepper

1 teaspoon baking powder

1 garlic clove, minced

3 tablespoons sliced green
   onions, divided

Olive oil, for frying

To make the lox sauce, in a small bowl, mix together the cream cheese, sour cream, lox, and green onion. Cover and refrigerate until ready to serve.

Preheat the oven to 200°F. Place a wire rack over a rimmed baking sheet.

To make the latkes, use the large holes on a box grater to shred the potatoes and onion. Put the potatoes in a bowl of cold water and swirl them around to get as much starch off the potatoes as possible. Drain the potatoes and place in a clean towel with the onion. Squeeze as much water out of the shredded vegetables as possible, then transfer to a medium bowl. Add the eggs, flour, salt, pepper, baking powder, garlic, and green onions and stir to combine.

Heat about ½ inch of oil in a skillet over medium heat until shimmering. Scoop the potato mixture into a ball a little larger than a golf ball and carefully place in the hot oil. Flatten with a spatula to make a 2- to 3-inch-wide latke. Add more latkes to the pan, keeping them about 2 inches apart. Cook for 3 to 4 minutes, until nicely browned on the bottom. Flip the latkes and cook on the other side for another 2 to 3 minutes. Transfer to the wire rack on the baking sheet and place the baking sheet in the oven to keep warm. Repeat with the remaining potato mixture.

Serve the latkes immediately with the sauce.

> **Stacy Lyn's Notes**
> The lox sauce can be made up to 1 week in advance and stored in an airtight container in the refrigerator. Latkes are also perfect with jellies and applesauce. If you have leftover latkes, store them in the refrigerator and reheat in a 350°F oven for 5 to 8 minutes, until heated through and crispy.

PORK SCALOPPINE WITH STONE-GROUND CHEESE GRITS AND GREENS

⟡ *Serves 8* ⟡

FOR THE STONE-GROUND CHEESE GRITS

5 cups water

1 cup stone-ground grits

3 tablespoons unsalted butter

½ teaspoon kosher salt

½ teaspoon freshly ground black pepper

½ cup grated Parmigiano-Reggiano cheese

¼ cup heavy cream (optional)

FOR THE GREENS AND PORK

Olive oil, for sautéing

1 large Vidalia onion, sliced

3 garlic cloves, minced

Leaves from 1 thyme sprig

3 cups finely chopped turnip greens and/or mustard greens

1 tablespoon red pepper flakes

¼ cup water

Kosher salt and freshly ground black pepper to taste

1 cup all-purpose flour

1 (1-pound) pork loin, sliced into 8 pieces and pounded to ⅛ inch thick

½ cup dry red wine, such as merlot or pinot noir

¾ cup chicken stock

3 tablespoons cold unsalted butter, cut into 3 pieces

½ cup toasted pine nuts, for serving

½ cup grated Parmigiano-Reggiano cheese, for serving

To make the grits, combine the water, grits, butter, salt, and pepper in a large stockpot. Bring to a boil, stirring constantly, then turn down the heat and simmer for about 30 minutes, stirring often. Turn off the heat and cover to keep warm.

Meanwhile, make the greens: Heat 1 tablespoon oil in a skillet over medium heat. Add the onion and sauté until almost translucent, about 8 minutes. Add the garlic and cook for 1 minute. Add the thyme leaves, greens, red pepper flakes, and water. Cover the pan, turn the heat down to medium-low, and cook, stirring often, until the greens have wilted, about 12 minutes. Season with salt and black pepper, then transfer the greens to a bowl. Wipe out the skillet.

Place a wire rack over a rimmed baking sheet. In a shallow dish, whisk together the flour, 1 tablespoon salt, and 1 teaspoon black pepper. Heat 2 tablespoons oil in the skillet over medium-high heat. Working in batches, dredge the pork slices in the flour, then place in the hot pan. Cook for 2 minutes, then flip the pork and cook for another minute. Transfer the pork to the wire rack and tent with aluminum foil. Add more oil as needed to cook the remaining pork.

Once all the pork has been cooked, turn the heat down to medium, add the wine to the pan, and simmer to reduce by half, about 4 minutes. (The wine will deglaze the pan, which allows the caramelized bits stuck to the bottom of the pan to release, creating added flavor.) Add the stock and simmer to reduce by half again, about 5 minutes. Whisk in the cold butter a tablespoon at a time. Season with salt and pepper and remove from the heat.

When ready to finish the grits, add the Parmigiano-Reggiano and cream (if using, for a smoother, creamier texture) to the grits and stir until combined.

Spoon some grits in the center of each serving dish, top with a piece of pork scaloppine and add greens and sauce on top of the pork. Garnish with toasted pine nuts and grated Parmigiano-Reggiano cheese.

Stacy Lyn's Note

You will want to have the cheese grits ready when you start to cook the pork. Covering them will keep them warm, but if you do need to reheat them, just add a little chicken stock and warm them over low heat, stirring to keep them smooth.

AUTHENTIC BANANAS FOSTER

❧ *Serves 6* ☙

8 tablespoons (1 stick) unsalted butter

1 cup dark brown sugar, firmly packed

1 teaspoon ground cinnamon

½ teaspoon kosher salt

½ cup heavy cream

6 ripe bananas, halved lengthwise, then halved crosswise

3 tablespoons banana liqueur

¼ cup rum or 2 teaspoons rum flavoring

½ cup toasted or candied pecans (page 229), optional

Vanilla ice cream, for serving

6 mint sprigs, for garnish

In a large skillet, heat the butter over medium heat until melted. Add the brown sugar, cinnamon, and salt and cook for about 2 minutes, until the sugar is dissolved. Pour in the cream and stir until combined. Add the bananas and cook, gently spooning the butter-sugar mixture over the bananas, for 5 minutes, or until the bananas are soft.

Remove the pan from the heat and carefully add the banana liqueur and rum. Place the pan back on the stove and shake it back and forth over the burner a few times to incorporate the rum into the sugar mixture. Be careful, as the pan will flame. If it doesn't flame, use a utility lighter or long match to ignite it. Carefully spoon the sauce over the bananas until the flame burns out, about 2 minutes.

To serve, divide the bananas into six bowls. Add a large scoop of ice cream over the bananas, then spoon some sauce over the ice cream. Top with pecans if you are using them and a sprig of mint. Or you can serve it like we do at our house: top with ice cream, give each person a spoon, and serve straight from the skillet!

New York Needs the South

For my fortieth birthday, Scott decided to take me to New York for the weekend, and I couldn't have been more excited. We spent several weeks planning what restaurants, plays, activities, and hotels we were going to visit, making travel arrangements and reservations, as well as packing our "casual chic" outfits. Finally, the day of departure arrived. I put on my favorite maternity pants and sweater, and hoped I'd have a little leg room on the airplane. I was six months pregnant with my seventh baby, so I looked and felt nine months pregnant! But hey,

yet, but seeing my "condition," they invited us to sit at the bar until then. To this day, Scott and I think they thought we were "testing" them—that we were food critics, disguised as a few backwoods Alabamians.

We'd never been treated so wonderfully in all our lives. Scott and I let the chef decide our menu. I don't remember everything I had, but I do remember it was remarkable, even my Italian version of a deconstructed peanut butter and jelly sandwich! Who knew? Even though I know it's not fair, I sometimes find

Enjoy where you visit but love where you are from!

even more reason to devour everything New York has to offer—which was *a lot*!

We arrived safe and sound in New York City. After a wild taxi ride to the hotel, we decided we'd be better off walking. Our destination was an Italian restaurant I'd been dying to try, and our reservation was less than an hour away. We set out making great time, but then the walk became . . . well . . . if you can imagine having a basketball filled with water sitting right above your hip bones and walking down a few questionable streets (very quickly), and the map you're using is playing tricks on you like a mirage of water in the distance, then you know how the walk became. "It's going to be worth it. It's going to be worth it," were the words I kept chanting. By the time we got to the restaurant, I thought I might be going into labor. The restaurant wasn't open

myself comparing the amazingly hospitable service of that restaurant to Alabama restaurants. The food and hospitality were certainly worth the walk!

The next night, since I had enjoyed the Italian food the night before and was still craving more, we found a quaint Italian eatery that I just had to try. I could smell the flavors from the door! We thought since we were going at an off time, we'd have luck getting in, but their reservations were booked solid for a month. After pleading with them a bit (and again playing the part of a very pregnant lady), we were seated. There was a bench that stretched the length of the room with a long table and chairs opposite the bench. Scott and I sat on the end next to the door. I don't think I could have gotten a better seat in the house. Just when I was starting to think maybe New

York was the place to be, I was reminded of all the reasons I actually love where I'm from more than anywhere in the world.

Across from us was a woman who was dressed to the nines, with perfect hair and a crisp work suit—the opposite of our casual chic tourist wear. She was everything that makes a seven-month pregnant lady feel about seventy months pregnant! When the waiter started heading her way though, I saw her face fall about fifteen stories to street level. When he placed a whole fish in front of her, the color drained out of her face completely. She had no idea what to do, or how to eat the fish. That's where being from Alabama came in handy. Our men know how to run a trotline, harvest the fish, fillet it or cook it whole, and eat it. (Scott even had a coworker bring a whole fish sandwich to work every day, eating the entire sandwich with only clean bones left when he was finished.)

The poor polished lady tried to cut the fish tail with her fork and knife, but the knife wouldn't go through the bones, and the fish fell right into her lap. She called the waiter in a panic. After he retrieved the fish, she placed an order that she "understood." We debated helping her, but her piercing looks were sharper than a knife, and I'm not sure she would have appreciated a few Southern hicks telling her what to do.

New York was everything I thought it would be, but I learned a lesson that surprised me—and may surprise a few New Yorkers: Alabama has everything I need and want for the good life. I'll forever love to visit the great places of the world, but Alabama is my home sweet home!

CRISPY SCORED FLOUNDER
WITH PEACH GLAZE
❧ *Serves 1* ❧

12 rosemary sprigs

1 lemon, thinly sliced

1 tablespoon olive oil

1 tablespoon unsalted butter, melted

8 garlic cloves, minced

1 (2-pound) trout or other flat fish, cleaned, fins trimmed

1 tablespoon kosher salt

1 teaspoon freshly cracked black pepper

½ cup peach preserves

1 tablespoon balsamic vinegar

1 teaspoon peeled and grated ginger

1 teaspoon cayenne pepper

Lemon and lime wedges

Preheat the oven to 450°F. Line a rimmed baking sheet with aluminum foil and coat it with cooking spray. Scatter the rosemary sprigs and half of the lemon slices over the foil for a bed under the fish.

In a small bowl, mix the oil, melted butter, and garlic together. Use a knife to score the fish diagonally, making about 8 slits about 1 inch apart, then brush the garlic butter mixture over the entire fish. Season the fish with the salt and black pepper and lay it over the rosemary and lemons. Cover the sheet with foil and roast for 20 minutes.

Meanwhile, in a small saucepan, heat the peach preserves, vinegar, ginger, and cayenne over medium heat until reduced by one-third.

Remove the fish from the oven and remove the foil. Spoon the peach glaze over the fish, then return it to the oven, uncovered, and roast for another 20 minutes, or until the fish is cooked through (145°F). Remove from the oven and brush more glaze over the top of the fish. Adjust the seasoning and serve with the remaining lemon slices, lemon wedges, and lime wedges.

Stacy Lyn's Note:
To eat the fish, pull the back side and belly side fins from the fish. With a knife, gently slice down the line of the spine from the head to the tail until you feel bone. On a flatfish, this will be in the center of the fish. With a fork or spoon, ease the fillet away from the spine, avoiding the bones and pulling the flesh from the spine outward away from the midline, revealing the spine and bottom fillet. There will be a rib cage toward the head of the fish. Lift the bones from the head end, easing the flesh off the bones as you lift the bones toward the tail. Lay the bones aside (to use for fish stock later) and you should see the bone-free bottom fillet.

CHAPTER 10

Southern Charm

"Did y'all win the championship football game last Saturday, Bill? Oh, by the way, this package is going to Boston, and I'd really like it to have those flower stamps if you have any back there. I know Daniel likes my berry jam, so will you take this home to him? And please do say hello to Pam for me, will you?" Bill may not have a chance to get a word in edgewise, but he'll sure know he's been touched with a little Southern charm . . . and that's always a good thing.

Southern charm is a way of life. Besides the accent, we are naturally curious, caring people who get to know the names and hobbies of those who serve us, and their families, or those we see on a regular basis. Sure, we often wrap around the world. They remember if you prefer blackberry jelly over strawberry jam, or if you would rather have cream-filled doughnuts than the traditional ones, and they'll make it their ambition to get what you like as soon as possible.

To make people happy is important, and laughter is such a big piece of that pie. Sure, laughing creates permanent smile wrinkles, but those wrinkles are welcomed. I believe that along with caring about people, it's the laughing and little bit of wit that's contagiously charming. Who doesn't love that?

Friendly, witty, and considerate, barring those who have crossed our family in some way, Southern charm is unmistakably appealing.

Southern charm can be a way of life, no matter where you live.

every one of those names and hobbies into one chatty conversation, but that's the fun of it!

When you meet someone with Southern charm, you will most likely be greeted with a toothy smile and a sincere question to get the conversation rolling. In less than five minutes, you will have divulged where you are from, where you live, if you have children, where they go to school, and their likes and dislikes. They'll instinctively know if you need a friend or a helping hand and will be there immediately for both. When they see you again, they will remember everything—because what looks like Southern charm on the surface boils down to people caring about other people.

Those with Southern charm go the distance to make sure *everything* has a special touch, from a hand-painted card or letter to the stamps they put on packages to be delivered

I have a psychology degree and love people-watching. Over the years, I have noticed that the people everyone wants to be around aren't the drop-dead gorgeous ones, or the ones who have some big successful job. It's the people who make others feel good about themselves—they are nice. And as my dad says, "It's nice to be nice." That's all there is to it. There's a lot of charm in that one little statement.

Maybe it's no surprise he also taught me this old saying: "You catch more flies with honey than with vinegar." That's also at the heart of Southern charm. To return good for evil and to be nice even when it's not natural. Being kind when it's not deserved. Paying attention to the details of a conversation. Making the small things special, smiling and making eye contact, and laughing are quintessentially the Southern way.

With Manners and Thankfulness, You Can Rule the World

I was fourteen years old when I ran my first campaign. I've never had so much fun as running for student council president of my junior high school. Friends helping with posters, handing out flyers, and laughing together as we created the craziest slogans to campaign by, and my favorite, choreographing a routine for after my speech to Michael Jackson's "Beat It"—these were just a few of the reasons for running.

Winning that election left me hungering for the next, in more ways than one. Besides

planning campaigns. And every sleepover required pizza. Not just any pizza, mind you, but a souped-up Domino's pizza. During my high school student council elections, it became clear that it was time to pull out the Southern charm, which this ambitious committee of girls could and did bring with no problems at all!

I made the call to Domino's but could barely hear the poor guy who answered the phone to take my order, because of all the shouting. "Pepperoni, pineapple, chicken, extra cheese, lots of bacon!" "What's your name? Are you the

Good manners and thankfulness are small things we do to have a big impact on others—it's the Southern way.

the free melt-in-your-mouth doughnuts our amazing lunch lady Gertrude provided us at our weekly meetings, experiencing the fulfillment of making a difference was addicting. I went on to run more campaigns, winning some and losing some through the years. But when I look back over all my campaigns, I don't think there was any one thing that ushered in a sure win; I believe the success came from treating others as I would want them to treat me and being thankful for each of their votes. The individuals in the class believed I knew them, or wanted to know them, and cared about them.

Through the years, I also learned having a sleepover was always in order for any strategic

head pizza maker? What's your favorite way to make the pizzas?" were some of the endless questions I asked our new friend, Jeff. We were ecstatic when he asked if we'd be interested in coming to Domino's to make our own pizza!

Yes! In our pj's and slippers, we loaded up in my friend's green Honda Accord and made our way to Domino's. Jeff met us at the door, and we began making creations that were otherworldly. I think we used an entire block of gooey cheese, at least a pound of bacon, and pepperoni, onions, and everything else available to us. That pizza was the best pizza I'd ever eaten. I wonder where Jeff is now; I've spent years learning to make a pizza that was as good as what we created that night, and I

would love to thank him for the inspiration he spurred in me through the years by allowing us free reign in Domino's!

The results of friendliness, manners, and caring are not just about what you can get. Winning campaigns or creating the best pizza ever is amazing, but this is about valuing the lives of all others. The true reward in making people feel special is knowing you have had a positive impact on the people in your world. That's actually how you rule! Learning that, and living it, is the Southern way.

PIZZA DOMINO'S STYLE
❧ *Makes 2 pizzas, serving 12* ❧

FOR THE PIZZA

4 cups bread flour

3 tablespoons granulated sugar

1 teaspoon active dry yeast

3 tablespoons dry milk

¼ teaspoon baking powder

1½ cups ice water

¼ cup vegetable oil

2 teaspoons kosher salt

1 cup cornmeal

8 ounces whole-milk mozzarella cheese, shredded (2 cups)

4 ounces provolone cheese, shredded (1 cup)

Toppings: sliced pepperoni, sliced mushrooms, cooked crumbled sausage, sliced onions, chopped cooked bacon, sliced black olives, sliced bell peppers, etc.

1 cup grated Parmigiano-Reggiano cheese

1 bunch basil, stems removed

FOR THE PIZZA SAUCE

1 (15-ounce) can tomato sauce

1 (6-ounce) can tomato paste

2 tablespoons Italian seasoning

1½ teaspoons kosher salt

2 teaspoons fresh oregano

½ teaspoon onion powder

½ teaspoon garlic powder

1 tablespoon light brown sugar, firmly packed

In a food processor fitted with the dough blade, pulse the flour, granulated sugar, yeast, dry milk, and baking powder until combined. With the food processor running, slowly add the ice water and process until the dough is combined, about 8 minutes. Let the dough rest for about 10 minutes. Add the oil and salt and process until the dough comes together and isn't sticking to the sides of the bowl.

Transfer the dough to an oiled work surface and knead for about 1 minute, then form into a very tight ball. Put the dough in a large oiled bowl, cover, and refrigerate for at least 24 hours or up to 4 days.

Dust the countertop with cornmeal. Divide the dough ball into two even pieces and form into tight balls, then dredge in the cornmeal. Place the dough balls at least 4 inches apart on the countertop, cover loosely with a kitchen towel, and let rest for 1 hour. (Alternatively, you can freeze the dough balls for 1 hour.) At the same time, preheat the oven to 500°F.

Meanwhile, make the pizza sauce. Mix all the ingredients in a large bowl until smooth.

Lightly grease a pizza pan or cast iron skillet and dust with cornmeal. Gently flatten one dough ball into a 10-inch disk. Leave the outer edge slightly thicker than the center of the disk. Transfer to the prepared pizza pan or skillet.

Using the back of a ladle or spoon, spread ½ cup pizza sauce in a thin layer over the surface of the dough, leaving a 1-inch border around the edge. Top with half of the mozzarella and provolone cheeses, along with your favorite toppings, then bake on the bottom oven rack for 10 minutes. Rotate the pan and bake for another 10 minutes, or until the crust is golden and the cheeses are melted. Top with half of the Parmigiano-Reggiano cheese and basil leaves. Repeat to make the second pizza.

Stacy Lyn's Note
You can store the sauce in an airtight container in the refrigerator for up to 1 week. I like to make a double batch and use the rest for spaghetti and meatballs later in the week.

Kill 'Em with Kindness

If my mom has said it once, she's said it a thousand times: "Kill 'em with kindness, Stacy. You know it always works." Anytime I felt someone was doing me wrong, this was her pat answer. It sounds kind of violent, but it's quite the opposite, and when put to use, has had a way of creating in my enemies a fondness toward me, and has created in me a fondness for them. Well, not always, but much of the time.

"Remember Mr. Jackson" has become synonymous with "Kill 'em with kindness" in my mom's list of advice idioms for me. Mr.

church. I couldn't help but think, why in the world would anyone lock the doors of a church?

Boy, were we in trouble, and I didn't know the half of it! We walked around to the front of the church, where the doors were unlocked and wide open, and proceeded as normal. But things were not normal. I saw Mr. Jackson talking to my parents; this was not good. Mom made a beeline straight for me with one of those knife-cutting looks—she's the best at those—and said I would not be singing in the choir that night, nor doing much of anything

It's better to kill your enemy with kindness than to walk around in bitterness. You never know what good may come from it!

Jackson was the father of one of my friends at church and what I once liked to call the "tattletale." If you've never been to a Baptist church, Sundays are filled to the brim with activities. Besides Sunday school and church in the mornings, there's choir practice, Training Union, which is an hour of training on what it means to be Baptist, and then church in the afternoon. I hated Training Union, and apparently so did a few of my friends, including Lexie, Mr. Jackson's daughter.

I was twelve, about to start junior high school, and didn't feel that I should have to go to Training Union, so a few of us decided to play hooky. Our mistake was hiding in a trailer behind the church. Who knew that when we tried to get back in, the doors would be locked? I sure didn't know they locked the doors of the

else for a while. But lo and behold, I saw that Lexie was going to be allowed to sing. Nothing happened to her. She didn't even get in trouble! What the heck? Why did Mr. Jackson see fit to get me in all this trouble if he wasn't even going to punish Lexie?

It's not that I wanted Lexie to get in trouble, but I sure felt singled out. My mom wanted the whole story once we got home. I was a horrible liar, and still am. I told her I went outside for a minute to get some fresh air and when the doors shut, I was locked out. She didn't call me a liar or punish me right then; she said okay, which was a little unnerving to me. I thought I got out of that one pretty easy . . . but she knew me better than that. She knew I'd crumble under the weight of the lie. All she had to do was wait it out.

Sure enough, she was right. I came clean and told her the entire truth, whereby she dealt out my punishment. I was to apologize to Mr. Jackson, the preacher, the Training Union teacher, and the choir director, and no fun for a month! So, all of this was doable, but what turned my stomach was having to apologize to Mr. Jackson, who in my mind had caused all of this! Of course, I really caused it, but I blamed him and still to this day don't understand why he made such a big deal about it to my parents when he didn't punish Lexie at all!

Mom shared with me that instead of carrying around bitterness, I should just "kill Mr. Jackson with kindness." I went to the limit with this assignment. I even brought him different kinds of doughnuts for several weeks in a row. I'm not sure if it was my kindness or the doughnuts that endeared him to me—maybe it was both.

I don't know where Mr. Jackson is today, but I'd sure like to thank him. I believe God wanted him to get me in all that trouble. During all of this, my mom said, "You are going to have to decide what you want to become. You are at a crossroads, and you can't split the fence. Get on one side or the other. If you choose the obedient side, you'll have to change your friends. Make your choice."

I did make my choice and have never looked back. Mr. Jackson changed my life for the better. I'm convinced I wouldn't be me without having had this experience. It was a true turning point in my life. Now, when someone purposefully sets out to harm me, I pull what Mom and I like to call a "Mr. Jackson." It works every time . . . well, almost.

TWO FAVORITE BLTS

Mama's Classic BLT
⤳ *Serves 4* ⤳

12 slices good-quality bacon (about 1 pound)

½ cup homemade or good-quality store-bought mayonnaise, such as Duke's or Hellmann's

8 slices good-quality white sandwich bread

Kosher salt and freshly ground black pepper to taste

4 iceberg lettuce leaves

2 medium vine-ripened tomatoes, sliced

Place a wire rack over a rimmed baking sheet.

In a large cast iron skillet, cook 6 slices of bacon over low heat. When the bacon begins to shrink and buckle, turn the bacon over and cook on the other side. Flip the bacon a few more times so that it cooks evenly on each side without burning. When the bacon is a little crisp and evenly browned on both sides, about 10 minutes total, transfer it to the wire rack to drain. Repeat with the other 6 slices of bacon.

Spread 1 tablespoon mayonnaise on each slice of bread. Sprinkle salt and pepper over the mayonnaise. Layer 3 slices of bacon, 1 lettuce leaf, and a few tomato slices onto 4 slices of bread. Top with the remaining slices of bread, mayo side down. Cut each sandwich on the diagonal and serve.

BLT All the Way
⤳ *Serves 4* ⤳

12 slices thick-cut applewood bacon (about 1 pound)

2 ripe avocados, halved and pitted

Juice of ½ lemon

2 tablespoons olive oil, plus more if needed

Dash Tabasco or other hot sauce

Kosher salt and freshly ground black pepper to taste

8 slices sourdough bread, lightly toasted

4 iceberg lettuce leaves

2 medium vine-ripened tomatoes, sliced

Set a wire rack over a rimmed baking sheet.

In a large cast iron skillet, cook 6 slices of bacon over low heat. When the bacon begins to shrink and buckle, turn the bacon over and cook on the other side. Flip the bacon a few more times so that it cooks evenly on each side without burning. When the bacon is a little crisp and evenly browned on both sides, about 10 minutes total, transfer it to the wire rack to drain. Repeat with the other 6 slices of bacon.

To make the avocado mayonnaise, scoop the flesh from the avocado halves into a blender. Add the lemon juice, olive oil, hot sauce, and ½ teaspoon salt and blend until smooth and emulsified. If you want the mayo looser, add a little more oil.

Spread 1 tablespoon avocado mayonnaise on each slice of toast. Sprinkle salt and pepper over the mayonnaise. Layer 3 slices of bacon, 1 lettuce leaf, and a few tomato slices onto 4 slices of toast. Top with the remaining slices of toast, mayo side down. Cut each sandwich on the diagonal and serve.

Stacy Lyn's Note
I was supposed to choose one BLT for this book, but I just couldn't do it. Both of these BLTs are crazy delicious!!

CHAPTER 11

Favorite Southern Holidays

The Busiest, Most **Chaotic** Fun Time of the Year

I've learned a few things through the years with the myriad of holidays and abundance of children. I can't do it all, all the time, and that's okay. There's a reason for every season, and making a big deal (or small deal) for those seasons ties strings of togetherness and gives you something wonderful to look forward to. And the biggest one: perfection is not the goal. One more time, perfection is not the goal.

My mother-in-law, Kay, like many Southern women, decorates for every holiday, even Saint Patrick's Day. She has an entire storage unit in her backyard carefully organized with containers labeled by holiday, full of dishes, napkins, tablecloths, special lighting, and other door in November. It inspires me. It seems to revive me . . . especially if there's a piece of homemade pie offered too—and there usually is!

I believe that's why Southern women like to decorate for every season. Each new holiday scene revives us. It gives us energy (and who doesn't need that?) as we look forward to that uninterrupted family time—the thing that really matters. I hope the excitement and energy I put into changing out the plates, decor, and even the menu for the holidays gives that same excitement, energy, and pep in the step to all those who experience it.

Of course, when holidays are such a big

The heart of the Southerner is revealed more during the holidays than any other time of the year: giving, kindness, making everything special, charity. Holidays are the heart of the South.

ornamentation to go with the holiday theme. Even though my father-in-law has to load and unload these boxes all year round, he loves it! He says it gives the house a little cheer and gives him something to look forward to. This works for them. I love that, and I especially love being the recipient of all their work and holiday excitement. We know they are doing it for us, the family, and it makes us closer.

Holiday decor always cheers me up. One of my very favorite things is stopping by a friend's home and being greeted with a flag hanging from the porch and red and blue petunias in pots flanking the door in July, or a colorful Thanksgiving wreath hanging on the deal, you want to work to make each year better than the year before, so there's a good kind of pressure that goes along with them. Some holidays tend to create a little chaos more than others. As much fun as Christmas is, preparing for it seems to give me an eye twitch every year. Don't get me wrong, I still love it, but all the decorating, cooking, wrapping, planning, and entertaining can put me into a frenzy. When that happens, I step back, remind myself that nothing is perfect, and then let the pressure be part of the season without letting it take over. I'm learning that feeling pressured just means I want the best holiday ever for the people I love.

Sometimes the overwhelm is a cue to let a few things go. Maybe you don't decorate every mantle this year, or you decorate minimally—there's beauty in simplicity, too, especially if that beauty is the smile on your face when you let go of the pressure. Remember that being happy is a gift to the whole family—a big one if you ask me. Sometimes, Southern women feel they have to do it all and do it all perfectly. Who came up with the rules of perfection? What is perfect? What you see in a magazine? Perfect for you (or me!) may be one nice arrangement in the middle of the table that sets the tone for everything, along with a nice spread of make-ahead dishes for the menu. By the way, most casseroles like dressing freeze beautifully. Sounds pretty great to me! Your family may vote to have the holiday simple every year because they love it so much.

The goal I reach for every holiday is to put the best food I can make on the table without being in a frenzy, and to have a happy, seasonal atmosphere that's conducive to fun and great conversation. If I accomplish that, I'm finer than a frog hair split four ways. You may have a different goal. Everyone does, but perfection doesn't need to be the goal. That will make you and those around you miserable in a New York minute.

With each bunny-themed table or cotton-covered Christmas village on the dressers in our homes, you'll be setting the stage for lifetime memories. Even though there's a ton of hustle and bustle surrounding many of the holidays, every minute spent creating the atmosphere and delicious food will be well worth it. Just remember to tie strings with those you love, perfection is not the goal, and always celebrate with a happy heart. You'll be giving yourself and your loved ones a mighty fine gift! Holidays are the heart of the South.

Thanksgiving and Christmas

⤳

"Whoa! Slow down, Dad. Whoa!" Mary shouted from the back as she gripped the trifle dish. Sounds of breaking glass came from the back of the Suburban, along with sliding casseroles and the swish of sweet tea. "OH. MY. GOODNESS. I think we are the only ones bringing the dessert. Turn around—we have to go back home and make another one!"

"Mom, we don't have any eggs to make the custard," is the news I get as I walk through the door. This can't be happening. Everything in Alabama is closed, but we do have chickens.

line. That's how we do it in my house, anyway. I think holidays may have been created as an excuse to eat desserts!

This kind of fiasco is indicative of my life surrounding Christmas. I always kid around saying that I need three more copies of myself during Christmas to get everything done. Every year, inevitably at the end of October, I get an eye twitch. Buying gifts for our immediate family is a full-time job, and I already have several of those! When January rolls around, I feel it's a wonder I made it through the holidays in one piece.

Thanksgiving and Christmas are a time to be thankful for Christ, but also a time to veer from the norm, create a little magic with those you love, and shower them with blessings, honor, and—let's not forget—*dessert*!

They aren't laying right now, but I'll say a prayer and send one of the kids to look all up under every chicken in the coop. "I got six eggs," Mary shouts, running wildly into the kitchen. "Hallelujah," Scott shouts as he starts the sponge cake.

Thirty minutes later, we head back out of the driveway with a brand-spanking-new trifle. Christmas miracles do indeed happen. If you're asking if desserts are really that important, the answer is a resounding yes. Some of us pass over the "healthy food," as my granny would call it, and go straight for the desserts. I claim it helps me eat less knowing I'm completely satisfied when I go through the healthy food

Why do we do this to ourselves? *The desserts.*

Not really. When I'm asking myself this question, it's Scott's grandmother, Greatma, who comes to mind. She used to go to the mall every day during the Christmas holidays because she "liked the energy." She was ninety-three at the time! It baffled me that anyone, especially a ninety-three-year-old, would want to drive in the traffic, park the car, walk for what seemed like miles to get into the mall, then walk around with people in a rush. She said, "It makes me feel alive." That's at the heart of why I keep at it and over the years have not been successful at scaling back at all—being with family and friends and having my heart that full makes me feel alive.

Even though it's all chaotic, the beautiful mess of it all has taught me to believe in miracles—whether they are big (like eggs magically appearing for the trifle) or small (like having cocoa with the girls while we wrap presents at the eleventh hour). We have a few Christmas traditions that keep me feeling more alive, which allows me to slow down for a moment and helps me celebrate the reason for the season. On Christmas Eve, which is my favorite part of Christmas, we eat my one-pot meal, venison bourguignon, then settle in the den outfitted in our pj's and enjoy homemade hot chocolate while Scott reads the Christmas story from the Bible. Then we watch *Elf*! This is something our entire family looks forward to, except when other movies are introduced—it can get a little rowdy to the true traditionalists.

As much fun as Christmas is, it may surprise you that Thanksgiving is our family's favorite holiday. It's centered more around the food and family without the hustle and bustle that Christmas can sometimes bring. It's a peaceful holiday. The family gets together, cooks the best of the best family recipes together, plays games, and hunts, and that's all we really need. It also kick-starts the holiday meals and desserts. (That may be the real reason!)

We enjoy Granny's cornbread dressing and giblet gravy, the moist chipotle-butter-garlic roasted turkey, mashed potatoes, cranberry chutney, pies loaded with pecans or sky-high meringues so much that we repeat the menu at Christmas. This menu needs to be served at least once a month, but especially

for Thanksgiving and Christmas. We may add a recipe or two or change up some of the ingredients from time to time, but we always return to the main attractions, and in their original form. Many of them are freezer-friendly too, making it a great make-ahead meal.

Houses decorated. Wafts of garlic turkey and homemade cookies floating through the halls. "Deck the Halls" tickling our ears as we hustle and bustle toward the big day. Even with the chaos, these are times to veer from the norm, create a little magic with those you love, and shower them with blessings, honor, and— let's not forget—*dessert*!

CHIPOTLE BUTTER AND GARLIC ROASTED TURKEY

Serves 10–12

1 (12- to 14-pound) turkey, rinsed and patted dry (reserve giblets and neck for Giblet Gravy, page 222)

Kosher salt and freshly ground black pepper to taste

1 cup (2 sticks) unsalted butter, softened

4 garlic cloves, minced, plus 1 head garlic

½ cup canned chipotle chiles in adobo sauce, minced

1 tablespoon chopped fresh rosemary

1 tablespoon dried oregano

1 tablespoon chopped fresh thyme

2 limes, quartered

Preheat the oven to 450°F.

Liberally sprinkle salt and pepper over the entire turkey, inside and out.

In a medium bowl, mix the butter and minced garlic with a fork until well incorporated. Stir in the chipotle chiles, rosemary, oregano, and thyme until well incorporated. Gently run your fingers under the turkey breast and thigh skin to loosen, then smear ¾ cup of the butter mixture under the skin and all over the outside of the turkey. Reserve the remaining butter mixture for basting.

Halve the head of garlic crosswise and rub the cut sides inside the cavity of the turkey. Stuff the cavity with both halves of the garlic head and the lime wedges.

Place the turkey, breast side up, on a rack inside a roasting pan. Fill the bottom of the pan with about 1 cup of water to keep the drippings from burning. Roast the turkey for 45 minutes, or until the skin is golden brown. Reduce the oven temperature to 350°F and continue to roast the turkey, basting with the reserved butter mixture every 30 minutes. If the pan gets dry, add more water. After the second hour of the turkey being in the oven, begin checking the temperature of the turkey every 15 minutes to keep from overcooking. The turkey is done when an instant-read thermometer inserted in the thickest part of the thigh registers 160°F.

Transfer the turkey to a cutting board and let rest for at least 30 minutes and up to 1 hour to allow the juices to redistribute. Reserve the turkey drippings in the pan to make Giblet Gravy (page 222). Carve the turkey and serve warm.

GIBLET GRAVY

❧ *Serves 12* ❧

Giblets and neck from 1 turkey, plus drippings from the roasting pan

4 cups chicken or turkey stock

2 cups water

4 tablespoons (½ stick) unsalted butter

¼ cup all-purpose flour

½ cup milk

2 large eggs, hard-boiled and chopped

½ teaspoon kosher salt

½ teaspoon freshly ground black pepper

Combine the turkey giblets and neck, stock, and water in a large saucepan and bring to a boil. Reduce the heat and simmer for 2 hours.

Place a fine-mesh strainer over a large bowl and drain the giblets. Transfer the giblets and neck to a cutting board and allow to cool. Remove the meat from the neck and chop the meat and giblets.

Melt the butter in a medium saucepan over medium heat. Stir in the flour and whisk continuously for 4 to 5 minutes. Slowly pour in the drippings from the roasted turkey and 2 cups of the giblet cooking broth, whisking constantly, and boil for 3 minutes. Add the milk and continue whisking until the mixture is thickened. Stir in the chopped boiled eggs, neck meat, and chopped giblets. Season with the salt and pepper and serve warm.

GRANNY'S ULTIMATE CORNBREAD DRESSING

❧ *Serves 12-14* ❧

8 tablespoons (1 stick) unsalted butter

1½ cups chopped onions

1½ cups chopped celery

6 cups crumbled cornbread

6 slices white bread, cubed

4 large eggs, beaten

3 cups chicken stock

2 (10.5-ounce) cans mushroom soup

1 tablespoon poultry or Creole seasoning

1 tablespoon kosher salt

½ teaspoon freshly ground black pepper

Preheat the oven to 350°F. Generously spray or grease a 9 x 13-inch casserole dish.

Melt the butter in a large skillet over medium heat. Add the onions and celery and sauté until the vegetables are translucent, about 8 minutes. Transfer to a large bowl.

Stacy Lyn's Notes

For this recipe, I make the cornbread with three packets of Martha White Buttermilk Cornbread & Muffin Mix. That's what my Granny used, so that's what I use, but the recipe works well with all kinds of cornbread recipes, so use your favorite! If you have leftover chicken or turkey, adding it to this dressing recipe creates an excellent main dish.

Add the cornbread, white bread, eggs, stock, mushroom soup, seasoning, salt, and pepper and mix thoroughly. Spoon the mixture into the prepared casserole dish. Bake for 35 to 40 minutes, until golden.

SOUTHERN PECAN PIE

❧ *Serves 8* ❧

1¾ cups chopped pecans, plus whole pecans for decorating

4 tablespoons (½ stick) unsalted butter, plus extra melted butter for brushing

½ cup dark corn syrup

½ cup light corn syrup

½ cup light brown sugar, firmly packed

2 tablespoons all-purpose flour

1 teaspoon vanilla extract

½ teaspoon kosher salt

4 large eggs

1 unbaked No-Fail Homemade Pie Crust (page 255)

Vanilla ice cream, for serving (optional)

Preheat the oven to 350°F.

Spread out the pecans on a rimmed baking sheet and roast for 5 to 7 minutes, until lightly browned. Check frequently as pecans can burn very quickly. Leave the oven on.

In a medium saucepan, melt the butter over medium heat. Add the dark corn syrup, light corn syrup, brown sugar, flour, vanilla, and salt and mix until incorporated and fully melted. Remove from the heat and allow to cool for 5 minutes.

Whisk the eggs into the syrup mixture and stir in the roasted pecans. Pour the mixture into the pie shell. Arrange whole pecans over the top of the pie.

Brush melted butter on the edges of the pie crust and bake the pie for 40 to 50 minutes, until the filling barely moves when shaken. If the pie is browning too quickly, place aluminum foil over the top of the pie until done.

Allow the pie to cool, then serve with vanilla ice cream if desired.

SWEET POTATO PIE WITH BOURBON-MAPLE WHIPPED CREAM

❧ *Serves 8* ❧

FOR THE PIE

1½ pounds sweet potatoes

4 tablespoons (½ stick) unsalted butter, melted and slightly cooled

½ cup cane syrup or dark corn syrup

½ cup light brown sugar, firmly packed

3 large eggs

1 cup cold heavy cream

¾ teaspoon kosher salt

¼ teaspoon ground cinnamon

¼ teaspoon ground ginger

½ teaspoon ground nutmeg

Pinch ground cloves

1 unbaked No-Fail Homemade Pie Crust (page 255)

FOR THE BOURBON-MAPLE WHIPPED CREAM

8 ounces cream cheese, softened

2 cups heavy cream

¼ cup maple syrup

1 tablespoon bourbon

2 tablespoons powdered sugar

1 teaspoon vanilla extract

Salted Maple Candied Nuts (page 229), for garnish

Preheat the oven to 350°F.

To make the pie, fill a large pot with water and bring to a boil. Add the sweet potatoes and boil for about 45 minutes, until a fork easily pierces through the potato. Transfer the potatoes to a colander and run cold water over them. When the potatoes are cool enough to handle, remove and discard the skins. Mash the sweet potatoes and measure out 3 cups (reserve any extra for another use).

In the bowl of a stand mixer fitted with the whisk attachment, whisk together the melted butter, syrup, brown sugar, and eggs on medium speed until well blended. Add the sweet potatoes, cream, salt, cinnamon, ginger, nutmeg, and cloves and mix until smooth. Pour the mixture into the prepared crust.

Bake for 40 to 50 minutes, until a toothpick inserted in the center comes out clean. Place the pie on a wire rack and allow to completely cool.

Meanwhile, to make the whipped cream, wash the mixer bowl and whisk attachment. In the bowl, whisk all the whipped cream ingredients on high speed until soft peaks form. Cover and chill for at least 20 minutes.

Cut the pie into wedges and serve with dollops of luscious whipped cream and a sprinkle of candied nuts.

SALTED MAPLE CANDIED NUTS
❦ *Makes 2 cups* ❧

1 tablespoon unsalted butter

2 cups roughly chopped pecans

2 tablespoons maple syrup

1 tablespoon light or dark brown sugar, firmly packed

Pinch salt

Line a rimmed baking sheet with parchment paper.

Melt the butter in a large nonstick skillet over medium heat. Add the pecans, syrup, brown sugar, and salt. With a wooden spoon, stir continuously for 3 to 5 minutes, until the nuts are completely coated and the nuts have soaked up the liquid. Transfer the nuts to the prepared baking sheet and spread them apart to cool. Store in an airtight container at room temperature for up to 1 month.

Stacy Lyn's Note
Sometimes I like serving candied nuts shiny, and sometimes I like them crystalized! The shiny glazed nuts feel a little more formal, while the crystalized ones have a sophisticated air, but more casual. If you want shiny candied nuts, stir them only occasionally as they cook; if you want them crystalized, stir them constantly before removing them from the heat.

CRANBERRY-ORANGE CHUTNEY
❦ *Serves 12* ❧

1 cup walnuts, chopped

12 ounces fresh cranberries

3 oranges, peeled, roughly chopped

¾ cup sugar

Preheat the oven to 350°F.

Spread out the walnuts on a rimmed baking sheet and roast for 6 to 8 minutes, until lightly browned. Remove from the oven and set aside to cool.

In a food processor, pulse the cranberries, oranges, and sugar until finely chopped. Pour the cranberry mixture into a bowl and stir in half of the roasted walnuts. When ready to serve, sprinkle the remaining walnuts on top.

Easter

When I was growing up, Easter was my second-favorite holiday, after Christmas. Everyone was dressed to the nines at church, and there was always a huge Easter egg hunt on the grounds. The winning egg usually had a nice prize, and I was determined to get it. Afterwards, we'd head home, where my grandparents would meet us for an Easter dinner of ham, deviled eggs, ambrosia, pineapple casserole, and, of course, carrot cake. My mom made a killer ham!

I don't prepare ham for any other holiday, but Easter just says ham to me. And obviously, favorite, a stuffed bunny. I'm a sucker for a stuffed animal.

We haven't been as elaborate with the kids' baskets, just because there are so many of them, but we've made up for that with some out-of-this-world decorating contests and egg hunts. Scott is an amazing artist and passed it on to our kids! I'd be scratching out a stick figure on the eggs, but you should see their designs and imagination manifested on these eggs.

Though Easter seems dreamy, neat, and picture-perfect enough, I must confess the

There's nothing a little ham with super deluxe fixings can't fix!

you can't have Easter without deviled eggs. Besides eggs representing new life—and tasting so dang good—we're always overloaded with them from the Easter egg competitions and hunts. Inevitably, we still find eggs hidden during the spring when we start cleaning the yard for the summer. If it's raining, we have our hunt indoors, then find the missed eggs much sooner once the house begins to stink of sulfur!

Besides believing in the Easter Bunny until I was sixteen (I'm just kidding, but my parents were very convincing), the Easter basket is another main reason I loved the holiday. Traditionally, Easter baskets are filled with hollow chocolate bunnies; yellow, pink, and purple Peeps; Jordan almonds, which are my mom's favorite; SweeTarts; and my

other side of that coin—and there's always another side. It reminds me of the scene in *Father of the Bride Part II* where George and Nina imagine very different visions of what it will be like raising another child. In Nina's mind's eye, she sees a pristine little girl, dress and bow perfect, skipping along and eating an ice cream cone. But George sees a holy terror screaming bloody murder and refusing to obey his father. I've shown you the beauty of Easter in the South. Now the reality, which is still in its own way sort of charming.

When we moved back from Birmingham, our first home in Montgomery was about a block away from my in-laws. The plan was for them to meet us at our house after church on Easter, so they were there when we pulled up. As soon as

we put the Suburban into park, the kids started flying out of the car. Kay, my mother-in-law, was stoked, thinking, "They just can't wait to see me! They're piling out at the speed of light." What she didn't see because the windows were fogged up from the humidity, among other things, was that our beagle, Icee, had just vomited all over the car. The kids were running because they were trying to escape! As soon as Kay opened the door to let two-year-old Howlett out, poor Icee flew out of the car, leaving a trail of vomit in his wake, and to top it all off, Howlett, God only knows how, had on Graylyn's patent leather Sunday Schools shoes . . . on the wrong feet! To this day, I cannot remember why Icee was in the car with us. But Kay took it all pretty well, especially when she saw the kids had all stayed in the yard to give her the hugs she wanted.

What a fiasco! Thankfully, we have great food to ground every situation, and Easter food is mighty fine in the South. There's nothing a little ham with super deluxe fixings can't fix!

SOUTHERN COCA-COLA GLAZED HAM

∾ *Serves 10–12* ∾

1 (7- to 8-pound) fully cooked, bone-in, spiral-sliced ham

¾ cup light brown sugar, firmly packed

1 (12-ounce) can Coca-Cola

¾ cup Dijon mustard

½ cup orange juice

Preheat the oven to 350°F. Line a roasting pan or 13 x 9-inch baking pan with aluminum foil.

Put the ham in the prepared pan.

In a medium bowl, whisk together the brown sugar, Coca-Cola, Dijon mustard, and orange juice. Pour the mixture over the ham and rub it into the slices of the ham.

Cover the pan with aluminum foil and bake on the bottom oven rack for 2½ hours, basting with the pan drippings every 30 minutes. Uncover and bake for another 30 minutes, or until the ham is browned. Remove the ham from the oven and let it rest in the pan for 10 minutes. Transfer to a serving platter and serve warm.

PINEAPPLE CASSEROLE

❦ *Serves 12–14* ❧

2 (20-ounce) cans crushed pineapple, drained, ¼ cup juice reserved

½ cup all-purpose flour

½ cup sugar

2 cups shredded sharp cheddar cheese

2 sleeves butter crackers, such as Ritz

8 tablespoons (1 stick) unsalted butter, melted

Preheat the oven to 350°F. Lightly grease a 9 x 9-inch casserole dish.

In a large bowl, mix the pineapple, reserved pineapple juice, flour, sugar, and cheese. Pour the mixture into the prepared casserole dish.

> ***Stacy Lyn's Note***
> This casserole makes it to the table on every family occasion. It's always a winner.

In a medium bowl, crush the crackers and mix with the melted butter. Sprinkle the cracker mixture over the pineapple mixture.

Bake for about 30 minutes, until the crackers are golden. Serve immediately.

CLASSIC SOUTHERN CARROT CAKE
with CREAM CHEESE FROSTING
❧ *Serves 16* ❧

FOR THE CAKE

3 cups all-purpose flour

2¼ teaspoons kosher salt

2 teaspoons ground cinnamon

1½ teaspoons baking soda

1½ cups granulated sugar

1½ cups light brown sugar, firmly packed

1½ cups vegetable oil

6 large eggs

4½ cups grated carrots (about 10 medium carrots)

2 cups coarsely chopped pecans or walnuts

FOR THE CREAM CHEESE FROSTING

1 pound cream cheese, softened

6 tablespoons unsalted butter, softened

8 cups powdered sugar

1 teaspoon vanilla extract

2 to 3 tablespoons orange juice, if needed

Preheat the oven to 350°F. Grease and flour a 9 x 13-inch baking pan.

In a medium bowl, whisk together the flour, salt, cinnamon, and baking soda.

To make the cake, in the bowl of a stand mixer fitted with the whisk attachment, mix the granulated sugar, brown sugar, and oil on low speed. Turn the speed up to medium and add the eggs one at a time, mixing well after each addition. Remove the bowl from the mixer and add the flour mixture in two batches, stirring until incorporated but not overworking the batter. Gently fold in the carrots and nuts.

Pour the batter in the prepared baking pan. Bake for 25 minutes, or until the cake is golden brown and begins to barely pull away from the side of the pan. Place the pan on a wire rack until completely cool.

To make the frosting, wash the mixer bowl and whisk attachment. In the bowl, mix the cream cheese and butter on medium speed until light and fluffy, about 2 minutes. Add the powdered sugar and vanilla and mix until completely incorporated. Add the orange juice if the frosting seems too thick.

Cover the top of the cake with the frosting. Refrigerate the cake for about 20 minutes, until the frosting is set.

Stacy Lyn's Note

Decorating this carrot cake is incredibly simple. I assign this task to my kids, and they've always been successfully creative. By mixing orange and/or green food coloring with leftover frosting and filling a piping bag with each color, small carrots can be piped onto the cake or one large carrot, whichever you prefer. Adding a few extra walnuts around the sides of the cake also makes the cake look festive.

SOUTHERN SPOON ROLLS

Serves 12

2 tablespoons lard

3 tablespoons sugar

1 cup hot water

2¼ cups all-purpose flour

1 large egg, beaten

1 teaspoon kosher salt

1 (¼-ounce) packet active dry yeast

In a large bowl, dissolve the lard and sugar in the hot water, then let the mixture cool to lukewarm. Add the flour, egg, salt, and yeast, pouring the salt and yeast on opposite sides of the bowl. Stir the ingredients together, then cover the bowl with a kitchen towel. Set aside until the dough doubles in size, about 1 hour.

Preheat the oven to 425°F. Grease a muffin tin.

Spoon the dough mixture into the prepared muffin tin, nearly to the top of each cup. Allow to rise again for 20 minutes. Bake for about 10 minutes, until golden brown.

New Year's Day

With the passing of each year, I am starting to realize the importance of maintaining traditions.

Holidays, and the traditions we associate with them, allow us to slow down and take a break from the "real world." Some people I know wouldn't ever have time in their constantly busy schedules for family if it weren't for traditions.

Every year when I was growing up, my family would celebrate New Year's Day during lunch at my grandaddy's house. In the South, the color of money, black-eyed peas because they represent pennies that when added together make for wealth, cornbread is the color of gold, and pork represents forward progress and good health—and who doesn't need good health? And pecan pie is so good it surely means something! The more you eat, the more prosperous you'll be in the upcoming year.

Hoppin' John, a mixture of sautéed onions, bell peppers, celery, and black-eyed peas served over rice, is also a must for the Southern family. We enjoy this dish throughout the year—it's

> ## I don't think there is any one right way to celebrate New Year's Eve or New Year's Day, except to eat as much black-eyed peas, collards, and pork as you can!

it's all about the food on New Year's Day, and we sure buried our faces in it. I loved seeing Grandaddy at the stove stirring the black-eyed peas, with the ham hock or the hog jowls floating in them and releasing that porky goodness. You could smell the cornbread baking in the oven, along with a delicious pecan pie. "Dinner's ready," Grandaddy would say in his monotone silky voice, and everyone lined up to pile on their plates. Once seated we all talked about how we were going to spend the money our good luck and good vittles would bring.

Southern superstition says that each item on the menu has meaning and must be eaten in quantity. We eat collards because they represent just that good. I always silently hope that the "magic" of what it promises in terms of prosperity works every time we eat it.

As far as holidays go, New Year's is much more laid back than other traditional winter holidays, and I love that. It's easy to plan for because everything is laid out for me. I know the complete menu, and the activities will be the same: playing games, reflecting over the past year, and looking forward to the new year ahead. There's usually a football game to watch, so everyone has something fun to do. After a hectic Christmas season, this feels like progress and optimism—which is exactly the point!

I know a lot of folks stay up to greet the new year on New Year's Eve, but Scott and I want to start the year off right by getting plenty of sleep and feeling up to eating a full meal on New Year's Day! It may seem boring to you, but I love our New Year's celebrations.

I don't think there is any one right way to celebrate New Year's Eve or New Year's Day, except to eat as much black-eyed peas, collards, and pork as you can! It welcomes prosperity and optimism—and it's the Southern way!

HOPPIN' JOHN
❧ *Serves 12* ❧

2 cups fresh heirloom black-eyed peas (about 1 pound)

8 ounces bacon, chopped, or 1 ham hock

2 teaspoons bacon drippings (if using ham hock)

5 celery stalks, chopped

1 Vidalia or other sweet onion, chopped

3 garlic cloves, minced

4 cups water or chicken stock, plus more if needed

1 tablespoon kosher salt

½ teaspoon freshly ground black pepper

⅛ teaspoon cayenne pepper

3 cups cooked long-grain white rice

Chopped green onions, for garnish

Chopped orange, red, or green bell pepper, for garnish

Soak the black-eyed peas in a large pot of cold water for 24 to 36 hours, occasionally skimming off the scum that rises to the top of the water. Halfway through the soaking time, rinse the peas and cover with water again. Drain the peas.

If you're using bacon, cook the bacon in a large pot over medium heat until crisp. Leave the bacon and about 3 tablespoons fat in the pan; pour off the rest of the fat. (If you are using a ham hock, heat the 2 teaspoons bacon drippings in a large pot over medium heat.) Add the celery and onion and sauté until soft, about 4 minutes. Add the garlic and cook for 2 minutes.

Add the black-eyed peas, water or chicken stock, salt, black pepper, cayenne, and ham hock, if using. Bring to a boil, then lower the heat and simmer, stirring occasionally, for 45 minutes to 1 hour, until the peas are creamy and tender. If the liquid evaporates, add more water. Adjust the seasonings.

To serve, spoon about ¼ cup rice into each bowl and top with the peas. Garnish with green onions and peppers. Serve with a side of fried cornbread.

> **Stacy Lyn's Note**
> If you don't have time to soak your peas, put them in a pot, cover with water, and bring to a boil. Turn off the heat once it reaches a boil and let the peas stand for 1 hour. Drain and proceed with the recipe.

SOUTHERN COLLARD GREENS

❧ *Serves 6–8* ❧

8 ounces bacon, finely chopped

1 onion, chopped

1 tablespoon minced garlic

2 pounds collards,
    stems removed

1 ham hock (optional)

2 cups dry white wine, such as
    chardonnay or pinot grigio

4 cups chicken stock

1 tablespoon kosher salt

1 teaspoon freshly
    ground pepper

¼ teaspoon red
    pepper flakes

In a Dutch oven, cook the bacon over medium heat until crisp. Transfer the bacon to paper towels to drain; leave the fat in the pan.

Add the onion to the fat in the pan and sauté until translucent, about 5 minutes. Add the garlic and cook for 30 seconds.

Add half of the greens to the pot and let them shrink, then add the other half. Add the ham hock (if using), wine, stock, salt, black pepper, and red pepper flakes. Bring the mixture to a boil, then lower the heat and simmer for 1 hour. Transfer the collards to a serving bowl and top with the bacon.

Independence Day

Fireworks. Excitement. BBQ. Grills. Watermelon. Pool parties. Hot summer sun. Kids playing in the sprinkler. Homemade ice cream churning. Laughter. Music. Fun. Lots of life. Ah, the sounds of the Fourth of July.

Patriotism runs deep in Southern veins. Even the mouths of babes hail "God Bless America." Churches sing "My Country 'Tis of Thee" and "America the Beautiful." We stand and salute to the national anthem with hand over heart with deep sincerity at every opportunity.

Celebrating the Fourth of July is quite an old Southern tradition, dating back to the beginning of our country. In the South right after the Revolution, dinners were held for Independence Day, which worked their way into outdoor BBQ celebrations, like we have today. At these events, the Declaration of Independence was sometimes read aloud. Now, how patriotic is that?

Our family smokes or grills almost every Fourth of July. We usually head out to the country and sit under the trees, play

Patriotism runs deep in Southern veins. Even the mouths of babes hail "God Bless America."

Perhaps my family's patriotism is derived from our Scotch-Irish roots of being incredible warriors protecting the sheep and land in the old country. Perhaps it's from being raised to defend hearth, home, and family at all costs. All I know is that we Southerners are extremely territorial, and anytime something threatens our well-being or the well-being of our loved ones, we bow up and fight. That includes the well-being of our nation.

Many of the men in my life have some affiliation with the military. My dad, a Marine. My stepdad, a Green Beret. My father-in-law, a colonel in the Air Force. Patriotism runs deep. Their loyalty, like so many others, to keep our country free, makes Independence Day that much more important to celebrate.

badminton, and take the kids riding all over the land in the back of the pickup truck. If it's not too hot here in Alabama, we fish too. We'll often invite the grandparents and cousins for fishing and a fish fry, or we'll BBQ ribs, make burgers, or even better, do both. If I remember, I like to put a few chickens in the smoker too for all-week celebrating.

Smack-dab in the middle of summer, the Fourth is hot and humid here in Alabama, to say the least, but it's still the perfect time to celebrate Independence Day. Everyone can be outside, fireworks are beautiful in the summer sky, and it's nice to sit back, recuperate from the busyness life can bring, and reflect on our freedom. And the food . . . need I say more?

BEST GRILLED BBQ RIBS
ℰ *Serves 6-8* ℈

FOR THE RIBS

⅓ cup light brown sugar,
firmly packed

¼ cup smoked paprika

2 tablespoons kosher salt

1 tablespoon freshly ground
black pepper

1 tablespoon garlic powder

1 teaspoon onion powder

1 teaspoon ground mustard

¼ teaspoon cayenne pepper

3 to 4 pounds spareribs

FOR THE BBQ SAUCE

½ cup ketchup

½ cup apple cider vinegar

½ cup light brown sugar,
firmly packed

1 tablespoon Dijon mustard

1 tablespoon smoked paprika

1 tablespoon garlic powder

1 tablespoon Worcestershire
sauce

2 teaspoons freshly ground
black pepper

1 teaspoon kosher salt

Alabama White Sauce (page
189), for serving (optional)

If using a gas grill, heat one burner or preheat to 200°F. If using a charcoal grill, stack the charcoal on one side.

To make the ribs, in a small bowl, whisk together the brown sugar, paprika, salt, black pepper, garlic powder, onion powder, ground mustard, and cayenne. Pat the ribs dry and remove the membrane. Rub both sides of the ribs with the dry rub mixture. Wrap the ribs in aluminum foil.

Place the wrapped ribs bone side up on the cool side of the grill. Cook for 1½ hours, then rotate the ribs 180 degrees and cook for another 1 to 1½ hours. After 2 hours of cooking, check every 30 minutes to see if the meat is pulling away from the bone. Remove the ribs from the grill.

Meanwhile, to make the BBQ sauce, in a medium saucepan, combine all the sauce ingredients and cook over medium heat, stirring frequently, until the mixture begins to thicken, about 7 minutes.

Heat the grill to 450°F by turning on all the burners of a gas grill or adding more coals to a charcoal grill and spreading them out evenly. Oil the grill grates. Unwrap the ribs and use a mop or brush to cover the ribs in the BBQ sauce, then place the ribs on the grill. Grill the ribs for 2 minutes without moving them, then flip them and grill for another 2 minutes, or until the sauce caramelizes. Remove the ribs from the grill and allow them to rest for about 10 minutes. Serve with extra BBQ sauce or Alabama white sauce.

CHAPTER 12

Banana Pudding
and Pies
A Reason to Fight in the South

Southerners have passion. We talk with passion, gesture with passion, and dream with passion. Passion goes two ways though. Sure, we may argue a little, but we love big—even our heated discussions occur because we love to see eye to eye with folks . . . and convince them we are right.

Some of our family's biggest arguments have been over the right way to prepare dessert, specifically banana pudding. Scott isn't to be reckoned with when it comes to banana pudding. He likes meringue; I like whipped cream. We each have half the family on our side, and there's no understanding between the two sides on this. Each believes without a

Once the banana pudding is made, you've never seen such expressions of fine accomplishment and fulfillment from both camps presenting "the best" banana pudding. Both sides pull out all the persuasive tactics they've ever known to convince the others that their team is indeed right. I'll tell you what. Even if one had a change of heart, pride would never allow them to admit it. They'd rather be a grasshopper in a henhouse than accept defeat. We certainly don't want anyone to get too big for their britches in this house!

It's all in good fun! It's our love language—the whole experience together . . . and the banana pudding. The laughter,

I believe the Southerner can be summed up in one word: passion. Passion for each other, manners, hospitality, home, holidays, and, of course, food.

shadow of a doubt they are right. The meringue lovers are purists, saying that banana pudding has always had meringue for the topping, while the whipped cream lovers say that it doesn't matter what came first, whipped cream is just better on banana pudding.

I wish you could be a fly on the wall. My camp is on one side of the kitchen, and Scott's crew is on the other, both with determination written on our faces, smack talk on our lips, and in hand-to-whisk combat with the "enemy" across the kitchen island. Someone might just "accidentally" let a little heavy cream or egg white fly from the bowl and make its way into the other's mixture.

fulfillment, and just plain fun in the kitchen together, and then each eating both troupes' creations with curiosity and anticipation—this always transpires into great conversation, and sometimes a new recipe, or new way of doing things.

The great thing about the South is that we aren't afraid to express our passion when we believe strongly in something. Often the results of the argument or heated moments are better than they ever would have been without the passion. For example, since I'm not convinced that banana pudding tastes better with meringue, Scott is always trying to make the meringue better, and he has

succeeded at that! So much that I may just flip sides before too long.

Of course, banana pudding isn't the only dessert that stirs the passions in the Harris household. Pies and cakes can be another source of contention: Should peanut pie be smooth or have broken bits of peanuts? Is coconut pie or chocolate pie better? Seven-minute frosting or buttercream? The list goes on and on. The thing is, with enough discussion, we will have created

the best desserts in the South before long. We will get to the bottom of the truth!

Passion, especially passion about food and family, gets me up in the morning. Mixing the two together on a regular basis—well, that just dills my pickle. I believe the Southerner can be summed up in one word: passion. Passion for each other, manners, hospitality, home, holidays, and, of course, food. Thank God for good ole Southern passion!

NO-FAIL HOMEMADE PIE CRUST

❧ *Makes 2 crusts* ❧

3 cups all-purpose flour, plus more for dusting

1 teaspoon kosher salt

¾ cup (1½ sticks) cold unsalted butter, cut into cubes

⅓ cup cold vegetable shortening, such as Crisco

6 tablespoons ice water, plus more if needed

In a food processor fitted with the steel blade, pulse the flour and salt to mix. Add the cubed butter and shortening and pulse until the butter looks like large peas. With the machine running, add the ice water. Pulse until the dough forms a ball; add more ice water if needed. Remove the dough from the processor and wrap in plastic wrap. Refrigerate for at least 30 minutes or up to 3 days.

> **Stacy Lyn's Note**
> I *love* this crust. It's my go-to crust for savory and sweet dishes. It works every time!

Cut the dough in half. Roll out one of the dough balls on a well-floured board, rolling from the center to the edge, turning and flouring the dough to make sure it does not stick. Continue rolling until the dough is 14 inches in diameter. Fold the dough in half over the rolling pin and place in a pie pan. Unfold and mold to the pie pan. If you aren't using the second dough, store it in a zip-top plastic bag in the freezer for up to 3 months. Thaw overnight in the refrigerator before rolling. Follow the desired pie recipe for filling and bake, or blind bake the crust!

To blind bake (partially or fully baking the crust without the filling), preheat the oven to 425°F. Line the pie shell with parchment paper and add pie weights to the crust. Fill the pie crust completely with the pie weights. Bake for 12 minutes or until the crust beings to brown, then remove the pie from the oven and lift the pie weights using the overhanging parchment paper. If you are partially baking the pie crust, pour the filling into the pie shell and continue to bake as per your recipe instructions. If you are completely blind baking the crust, place the crust back into the oven and cook for about 5 minutes, until the entire pie is golden. Remove the crust from the oven and allow it to come to room temperature, then follow the instructions for the pie recipe.

> **Stacy Lyn's Note**
> I use dried beans or dried rice as a substitution for pie weights. After using them, I keep the in a mason jar labeled pie weights. It works beautifully!

FAVORITE BANANA PUDDING
❦ *Serves 6–8* ❧

FOR THE BANANA PUDDING
3 cups milk

4 large egg yolks

1 cup granulated sugar

⅓ cup cornstarch

⅓ cup unsalted butter, cut into 6 pieces

2 teaspoons vanilla extract

Pinch kosher salt

FOR THE WHIPPED CREAM
2 cups heavy cream

½ teaspoon vanilla extract

6 tablespoons powdered sugar

FOR ASSEMBLY
1 (11-ounce) box vanilla wafers, 1 ounce reserved and crushed for garnish

5 ripe bananas, sliced

To make the pudding, in a large bowl, whisk together the milk and egg yolks.

In a medium saucepan, whisk together the granulated sugar and cornstarch over medium heat. Begin to slowly whisk the milk and egg mixture into the saucepan. Bring the mixture almost to a boil and whisk continuously until thickened, about 8 minutes. Remove from the heat.

Add the butter, one tablespoon at a time, stirring constantly and allowing each one to melt completely before adding the next. Add the vanilla and salt and stir to combine.

To make the whipped cream, in the bowl of a stand mixer fitted with the whisk attachment, whip the cream on high speed until it's foamy and has increased in volume, 3 to 5 minutes. Add the vanilla and then gradually add the powdered sugar and continue to beat until soft peaks form.

To assemble, in a large bowl or trifle dish, arrange a layer of vanilla wafers, then one-quarter of the bananas. Spoon one-quarter of the custard over the bananas, then top with one-quarter of the whipped cream. Repeat to make three more layers. Top with the reserved crushed wafers.

Stacy Lyn's Note

I love using all sizes of mason jars for banana pudding. Layer in the same order, and if you are eating the banana pudding right away, make the final layer a big dollop of whipped cream topped with whole or crumbled wafers. If you are saving for later, or are traveling with the pudding in a cooler, leave off the top layer of whipped cream, but leave ⅛ inch headspace at the top of the jar, and place the lids on. Once ready to serve, remove the lids and top with whipped cream and wafers!

Stacy Lyn's Note
 If you master the custard base of this recipe, you will be able to make banana pudding, coconut cream pie, butterscotch pie, chocolate pie, peanut butter pie . . . well, you get the drift!

COCONUT CREAM PIE

❧ *Serves 6–8* ❧

FOR THE COCONUT CREAM PIE

3 cups milk

4 large egg yolks

1 cup granulated sugar

⅓ cup cornstarch

⅓ cup unsalted butter, cut into 6 pieces

2 teaspoons vanilla extract

Pinch kosher salt

2 cups sweetened flaked coconut, divided

1 baked No-Fail Homemade Pie Crust (page 255)

FOR THE WHIPPED CREAM

2 cups heavy cream

6 tablespoons powdered sugar

½ teaspoon vanilla extract

To make the pie, in a large bowl, whisk together the milk and egg yolks.

In a medium saucepan, whisk together the granulated sugar and cornstarch over medium heat. Begin to slowly whisk the milk and egg mixture into the saucepan. Bring the mixture almost to a boil and whisk continuously until thickened, about 8 minutes. Remove from the heat.

Add the butter, one tablespoon at a time, stirring constantly and allowing each one to melt completely before adding the next. Add the vanilla, salt, and 1¾ cups of the coconut and stir to combine. Pour the custard into the pie crust. Cover with plastic wrap, making sure the wrap is touching the custard, and cool on a wire rack for about 30 minutes, then refrigerate until set, about 3 hours.

Meanwhile, preheat the oven to 350°F.

Scatter the remaining ¼ cup coconut on a rimmed baking sheet pan and bake for 5 to 6 minutes, until the coconut is lightly toasted, turning the pan and stirring the coconut once during the baking time. Remove from the oven and cool.

To make the whipped cream, in the bowl of a stand mixer fitted with the whisk attachment, whip the cream on high speed until it's foamy and has increased in volume, 3 to 5 minutes. Add the vanilla and then gradually add the powdered sugar and continue to beat until soft peaks form.

Remove the plastic wrap from the pie and spread the whipped cream all over the top. Sprinkle with the toasted coconut.

ULTIMATE PEANUT PIE

∾ *Serves 6–8* ∾

1 vanilla bean

⅓ cup dark brown sugar, firmly packed

2½ tablespoons all-purpose flour

¼ teaspoon ground cinnamon

¾ teaspoon kosher salt

¼ teaspoon cayenne pepper

3 large eggs, beaten

1 cup light corn syrup

2 teaspoons apple cider vinegar

4 tablespoons (½ stick) unsalted butter, melted

2 cups dry-roasted peanuts

1 baked No-Fail Homemade Pie Crust (page 255)

Ice cream or vanilla whipped cream, for serving

Preheat the oven to 350°F.

Split the vanilla bean lengthwise and scrape the seeds into a medium bowl. Add the brown sugar, flour, cinnamon, salt, and cayenne and whisk until well combined. Add the beaten eggs, syrup, vinegar, and butter and whisk until well combined.

Pour the peanuts into the pie crust. Pour the filling over the peanuts and shake just a bit to get rid of any air bubbles in the mixture.

Bake for about 40 minutes, until set. Allow to cool for at least 10 minutes. Serve with ice cream or vanilla whipped cream.

Acknowledgments

The support, effort, love, patience, and hard work of so many people made my vision a reality.

A big thank-you to my homebase team. Scott, for encouraging me to go after my dreams and pushing me further than I think I can go. I'm so glad I get to do life with you. Thanks to my amazing and talented assistants, Graylyn, Mary Elizabeth, Anna Julia, and Milly for endless recipe testing, errand running, and especially for sending me to my room for two weeks before my deadline to write. Thanks to Becca for doing everything and anything needed during the chaotic production of the book. Thanks to Forrest, Hampton, Howlett, and Abbi for tirelessly moving tables, props, fetching ice for the melting ice teas, taste testing all the recipes, and waiting patiently for photographs to be taken before dinner is served. Thanks to my dad, Wayne, for taking me fishing and my mother, Paula, for teaching me to be strong. And of course, thanks to my grandmother, Gray, for sharing her love language with me.

Thanks to everyone at Hachette for making the writing and production of this book seamless and one of the biggest joys of my life. I'd like to give a special thank-you to my editor Jeana Ledbetter, who gently and patiently walked me through every process, made my dream a reality, and made this adventure rewarding—I can't imagine ever working on any book without you. Thanks to creative director Kristen Andrews for creating a beautiful work of art; to Stacey Reid for your meticulous attention to the copy and recipes in the book; to Ashley Prine for designing such a gorgeous book.

A huge thank-you to my friend and colleague Bryan Frasher. You are a true visionary. Thanks for always encouraging me to see the bigger picture, believing in me, and keeping me grounded and on track.

Thanks to Justin Nekoufar and the Mindvolt team for believing in this project when it was in its infancy. Thank you Jody Frank for joyfully keeping my blog running while I was immersed in this book. You are a wonderful friend. Thank you Karen Longino for believing in this project and bringing it to Hachette.

Thank you to Sherry Holding, my very dear friend, for patiently listening to my vulnerabilities and insecurities and always being such a bright spot in my life! What a friend!

A huge thanks to all of you who watch my shows, watch my videos, follow me on social media, comment on my posts, come to my events, and read my books and blog. How can I thank you enough? Your encouragement keeps me writing. This would be impossible without you.

And lastly, thank you, Southern people. You are the reason the South is great and worthy to be written about. Thanks for your hospitality, kindness, and generosity!

APPENDIX A

Recipes by Course

Often, I need bread or an extra side dish to go with my meal and want to be able to find it fast. I want this book to be easy for you to find what you are looking for, so I've listed the recipes in the book by course. I hope this helps make your life easier and more fun in the kitchen!

Stacy Lyn's Meal Ideas

There are times when I want to fly by the seat of my pants and put together a meal as it comes to me in the kitchen. Then there are other days when I want someone to lay out exactly how the meal should go so I can just enjoy the process of cooking. For those days, I'm offering up ideas of how to pair the recipes in these books. Enjoy.

THE QUINTESSENTIAL SOUTHERN MEAL
- Granny's Southern Fried Chicken (page 9)
- Disappearing Deviled Eggs (page 176)
- Southern Collard Greens (page 245)
- Southern Spoon Rolls (page 239)
- Sweet Iced Tea (page 40)
- Southern Pecan Pie (page 225)

VEGETABLE PLATE
- Squash Casserole (page 30)
- Fried Green Tomatoes (page 33)
- Pineapple Casserole (page 235)
- Hoppin' John (page 242)
- Fried Jalapeño Cornbread (page 10)

OUTDOOR BBQ PARTY
- Best-Ever Smoked Chicken with Alabama White Sauce (page 189)
- Best Grilled BBQ Ribs (page 249) with Squash Relish (page 78)
- Double-Fried French Fries (page 136)
- Ambrosia (page 179)
- Homemade Peanut Butter Ice Cream (page 186)
- Watermelon Lemonade (page 43)

GAME NIGHT AT HOME
- Fried Cheddar Jalapeño Balls (page 23)
- Parmesan Fried Chicken Wings with Honey-Garlic Drizzle (page 112)
- Salted Maple Candied Nuts (page 229)

MOVIE NIGHT
- Pizza Domino's Style (page 208)
- Crispy Fried Onion Rings (page 29)
- Kitchen Sink Icebox Cookies (page 48)
- Peach Tea (page 44)

LUNCHEON
- Old-Fashioned Chicken Salad (page 123)
- Pimiento Cheese with Green Olives (page 120)
- Hummingbird Cake (page 58)

SUNDAY LUNCH
- Poppy Seed Chicken (page 52)
- Hoppin' John (page 242)
- Cranberry-Orange Chutney (page 229)
- Southern Spoon Rolls (page 239)

FRIENDS AND FAMILY NIGHT
• Ultimate Pot Roast and Creamy Great Northern Beans (page 103)

• Cornmeal Fried Okra (page 116)

• Southern Collard Greens (page 245)

• Bacon Cheddar Biscuits (page 124)

• Favorite Banana Pudding (page 256)

DATE NIGHT
• Roasted Tomato Soup with Grilled Cheese Sandwich Croutons (page 80)

• Cajun Shrimp and Grits Cakes (page 20)

• Bourbon Bread Pudding (page 130)

ANNIVERSARY
• Best Crab Cakes (page 148)

• Dill Pickle Tartar Sauce (page 152)

• Pork Scaloppine with Stone-Ground Cheese Grits and Greens (page 194)

• Authentic Bananas Foster (page 196)

LUNCH WITH THE KIDS
• Two Favorite BLTs (page 212)

• Mississippi Mud Cake (page 93)

**WINTER DINNER
(THAT MEANS LUNCH IN THE SOUTH)**
• Granny's Vegetable Soup . . . with Beef (page 90)

• Pimiento Cheese with Green Olives (page 120)

• Old-Fashioned Pound Cake (page 55)

GAME NIGHT
• Applewood Bacon–Wrapped Venison Steaks with Brown Butter Herb Sauce (page 159)

• Crunchy, Creamy Parmesan Roasted Potato Wedges (page 105)

• Southern Collard Greens (page 245)

• Cappuccino Cake (page 63)

• Homemade Peanut Butter Ice Cream (page 186)

SUPPER FOR A CROWD
• Fried Cheddar Jalapeño Balls (page 23)

• Stacy Lyn's Award-Winning Chili (page 173)

• Bacon Cheddar Biscuits (page 124)

• Caramel Cake (page 16)

TAILGATE
• Ultimate Bacon Pepper Burgers with Cheddar and Remoulade (page 14)

• Best Fried Pickles (page 115)

• Disappearing Deviled Eggs (page 176)

• Kitchen Sink Icebox Cookies (page 48)

• Favorite Banana Pudding (in mason jars) (page 256)

FISH FRY
• Authentic Red Beans and Rice (page 74)

• Southern Cornmeal-Crusted Catfish (page 146)

• Creamy Comeback Sauce (page 153)

• No-Fail Jalapeño Cheddar Hush Puppies (page 150)

• Double-Fried French Fries (page 136)

• Mixed Berry Iced Tea (page 47)

Index

provolone cheese, in Pizza
Domino's Style, 208
puddings
Bourbon Bread Pudding, 130
Favorite Banana Pudding,
256

Q

Quail, Red Pepper Jelly-Basted
Grilled, with Caramelized
Peaches and Figs, 162
quintessential Southern meal,
recipes, 266

R

rabbit, in Brunswick Stew, 170
raisins
in Bourbon Bread Pudding,
130
in Lane Cake, 61
Red Beans and Rice, Authentic,
74
Red Pepper Jelly, 163
Red Pepper Jelly–Basted Grilled
Quail with Caramelized
Peaches and Figs, 162
relishes
Green Tomato Chowchow,
77
Squash Relish, 78
Remoulade, Ultimate Bacon
Pepper Burgers with Cheddar
and, 14
rib eyes, in Steak Frites with
Roquefort Butter, 135
rice
Authentic Red Beans and
Rice, 74
in Hoppin' John, 242
Ritz crackers
in Pineapple Casserole, 235
in Poppy Seed Chicken, 52
in Squash Casserole, 30
Roasted Potato Wedges, Crunchy,
Creamy Parmesan, 105
Roasted Tomato Soup with
Grilled Cheese Sandwich
Croutons, 80
Roasted Turkey, Chipotle Butter
and Garlic, 221
Roquefort Butter, Steak Frites
with, 135

S

salads
Ambrosia, 179
Old-Fashioned Chicken
Salad, 123
Summer Panzanella, 83
Salted Maple Candied Nuts, 229
Shakshuka, 156
Shrimp and Grits Cakes, Cajun, 20
side dishes. *See* vegetables and
side dishes
Smoked Chicken with Alabama
White Sauce, Best-Ever, 189
smoked sausage, in Authentic
Red Beans and Rice, 74
soups
Granny's Vegetable Soup . . .
with Beef, 90
Roasted Tomato Soup with
Grilled Cheese Sandwich
Croutons, 80
sourdough bread
in BLT All the Way, 212
in Roasted Tomato Soup
with Grilled Cheese
Sandwich Croutons, 80
in Summer Panzanella, 83
Southern charm, about, 205–7
Southern Coca-Cola Glazed
Ham, 232
Southern Collard Greens, 245
Southern Cornmeal-Crusted
Catfish, 146
Southern hospitality, about, 37, 51
the arsenal, 38
Southern meal, quintessential,
recipes, 266
Southern men, about, 182–83
Southern Pecan Pie, 225
Southern Spoon Rolls, 239
Southern women, about, 101–2
Spoon Rolls, Southern, 239
Squash Casserole, 30
Squash Relish, 78
Stacy Lyn's Award-Winning
Chili, 173
Steak Frites with Roquefort
Butter, 135
Steel Magnolias (movie), 167
Stew, Brunswick, 170
Strawberry Cake with Strawberry
Buttercream Frosting, 138

Sugar Daddy Lollipop, 168
Summer Panzanella, 83
summer squash, Squash Relish,
78
Sunday dinner
about, 12–13
Caramel Cake, 16
Ultimate Bacon Pepper
Burgers with Cheddar and
Remoulade, 14
Sunday lunch, recipes, 266
Sweet Iced Tea, 40
in Mixed Berry Iced Tea, 47
in Peach Tea, 44
sweet onions. *See* Vidalia onions
Sweet Potato Pie with Bourbon-
Maple Whipped Cream, 226

T

tailgating
about, 110–11
recipes, 267
Tartar Sauce, Dill Pickle, 152
Thanksgiving
about, 219
Chipotle Butter and Garlic
Roasted Turkey, 221
Cranberry-Orange Chutney,
229
Giblet Gravy, 222
Granny's Ultimate
Cornbread Dressing, 222
Salted Maple Candied Nuts,
229
Southern Pecan Pie, 225
Sweet Potato Pie with
Bourbon-Maple Whipped
Cream, 226
toffee bits, in Kitchen Sink Ice
Box Cookies, 48
tomatoes. *See also* green
tomatoes
in Granny's Vegetable
Soup . . . with Beef, 90
Roasted Tomato Soup with
Grilled Cheese Sandwich
Croutons, 80
in Shakshuka, 156
in Stacy Lyn's Award-
Winning Chili, 173
in Summer Panzanella, 83
in Two Favorite BLTs, 212

About the Author

Southern lifestyle guru, television host, celebrity chef, best-selling author and speaker Stacy Lyn Harris wants her readers to pull up a chair, hear some funny and poignant stories, and incorporate her unfussy, delicious recipes into their special occasions and daily life.

"I don't go to my home and kitchen expecting perfection," Harris writes. "It's simply the place I go to return to what matters most: my family, my faith, and spending my days at home in the South. Time I spend cooking is time spent loving."

In addition to being a best-selling author of three books and host of *The Sporting Chef* on the Outdoor Channel, Harris is also the founder of the popular Stacy Lyn Harris blog. The Alabama native and mother of seven has grown a following with her simple approach to sourcing and preparing meals—often including wild game and ingredients from her garden.

Harris grew up with career-minded parents, so she has long known the importance of fast, accessible meals. Her grandmother always told her: "Food is more than just something to eat; relationships stick when built around a table of good-quality fresh food."

Harris got her law degree, got married, and started practicing. Her new husband was passionate about hunting, and Harris was anxious to find ways to connect with him and his hobby. His passion became her passion, and she took aim at discovering the tastiest ways to prepare his harvest.

Her writing and television career evolved with her family and their homesteading journey. Harris's experience on the land led to an arsenal of information about wild game, sustainability, cooking, and gardening, which she shared in her first four cookbooks: *Tracking the Outdoors In* (2011), *Wild Game: Food for Your Family* (2012), *Recipes & Tips for Sustainable Living* (2013), *Stacy Lyn's Harvest Cookbook* (2016) and her DVD *Gourmet Venison: Tasty Field to Table Recipes* (2013).

She scored the hosting position on *The Sporting Chef* TV show and was dubbed "a new breed of cook" for creating meals that are natural, sustainable, and delicious.

Through multiple cookbooks and cooking shows celebrating Southern charm, lifestyle, and seasonal, fresh protein, Harris is showing the world that Southern culture is more than "bless your heart" with a side of sweet tea.

It's also rich with recipes for a happy life.

"*Love Language of the South* beautifully, and deliciously, celebrates the table of what I believe is America's truest cultural food genre. The food of the American Southeast, with all its influences from our first peoples, the Caribbean, Africa, and western Europe, is American food. Stacy Lyn Harris's stories, recipes, and love of the outdoors, from field to stream to gardens, makes this book a must for every food lover."

—**Andrew Zimmern**, chef, author, teacher

"No matter where you're from, Stacy Lyn offers something for everyone. She lets us into her life in a very personal way and serves up some truly unique takes on the Southern-cooking staples that have been created through generations of love. I loved this book and I'm totally going to steal some of these recipes!"

—**Nick Hoffman**, country music artist and television host

"From 'Sunday Dinners' to 'Compassion in a Casserole,' love remains the theme, and food is always front and center. Stacy Lyn's recipes are dead-on and leave you inspired to gather friends and family and feed them well."

—**Carla Hall**, author and television host

"*Love Language of the South* is a complete guide that deep dives into the souls of us Southerners. Stacy Lyn captured all the feels in this wonderful tribute wrapped in faith and family! Stacy Lyn beautifully catches the true nostalgia of Southern heritage in a way that brought back every memory and aroma from my own grandmother's farm kitchen."

—**David Bancroft**, chef, owner of Acre and Bow & Arrow

"Whether you have ties to the South or not, Stacy will show you how to ooze a love language of delicious food around a welcoming family table. Just as this unique book has revived Southern charm in our New England home, it will connect lives and loved ones, across geography and generations, around the goodness of real food, done right."

—**Michelle Visser**, host of the *Simple Doesn't Mean Easy* podcast, author of *Sweet Maple*, and creator of the award-winning blog SoulyRested.com

"God, family, and country are the foundation of this nation's values. A great place to build and strengthen that foundation is around the kitchen table sharing delicious meals with the people you love—Stacy Lyn shows you how."

—**Craig Morgan**, country music hitmaker, author, celebrated outdoorsman, and Army veteran

"In her signature style, Stacy draws you into her world and causes you to feel like you're sitting at her table enjoying a glass of sweet tea. Her elegant, yet simple, recipes are accessible to everyone, and I can't wait to start whipping them up in my prairie kitchen."

—**Jill Winger**, author of *Old-Fashioned on Purpose* and *The Prairie Homestead Cookbook*

"Stacy Lyn Harris has shown us how to approach life, gardening, cooking, family, celebrations and how to live by the rhythm of Mother Earth, respecting each season and its bounty, its opportunity, and the hope of a life well lived. Bravo on your new book, SLH. . . . you make the world a better place, and we are grateful."

—**Chris Hastings**, owner and executive chef of Hot & Hot Fish Club and OvenBird, and winner of the James Beard Award for Best Chef in the South

"*Love Language of the South* approaches hosting and entertaining with casual reverence and a bit of whimsy. From formal dining menus and memories associated with passed-down favorites, Stacy Lyn's book offers an approachable guide to serving up some of the South's finest dishes. Readers will be encouraged to host their own gatherings, and feel confident that they, too, can leave pretense at the door and invite family and friends to join them around the table."

—**Anna Hartzog**, editor of *Entertain & Celebrate*